国际商务系列教材
Series of International Business

丛书主编：张立玉

国际商务礼仪

张立玉　著

WUHAN UNIVERSITY PRESS
武汉大学出版社

国际商务系列教材编委会

丛书主编

张立玉

丛书编委（按姓氏音序排列）

岑　粤　陈珞瑜　邓之宇　何明霞　贾　勤

雷　静　吕　昊　宁　毅　闫立君　杨　快

张立玉

序

随着商业经济和信息技术的飞速发展，以及经济全球化的进程加速，社会活动的各个层面都不可避免地趋向国际化，各种行业中的国际交流活动也日益频繁，商务交往手段越来越新颖化、多样化。商务活动已经不再局限于卖出单向交流，而是由内向外——从公司内部的运营到商场的服务，从个人的专业知识、才能到言行举止，达到全方位的人际交流。而英语作为其中最重要的信息载体之一，已成为现代国际社会各个领域中使用最广泛的语言，其重要性日益突出。

"商务英语"的概念来自于英文译文 Business English，而英文中"business"一词并不仅仅对应汉语"商务"（理解为生意或经营业务）概念，而是涵盖了所有非私人活动的社会公众活动。所谓"商务"，是指围绕贸易、投资等各类经济、公务和社会活动，包括贸易、金融、营销、旅游、新闻、法律、外事等领域。随着近年来中国的政治和经济实力不断的提升，特别是中国加入世界贸易组织以来，中国经济以前所未有的深度和广度继续对外开放，日益融入到区域经济和全球经济一体化的框架中，人们需要学习，了解更多的国际商务知识，熟悉国际商业规范，拥有较强的跨文化交际能力以便能直接参与国际合作与竞争。

目前国内人才市场对口径宽、适应性强的复合型英语人才需求旺盛。商务部的一项调查显示，我国急需高素质、复合型、具有较强国际竞争力的高级商务英语人才。调查预测未来二三十年内，高级商务英语人才的需求量将成倍增长。商务英语是一门交叉学科，涵盖了应用语言学和商科等诸多学科，商务英语人才也由于口径宽、适用性强而备受人才市场青睐。由此可见，随着我国经济的日益开放和跨越式发展，社会对外语人才的需求已经呈现出新的变化，单一的"英语基础技能+英美文学知识"培养方式已无法满足社会经济发展的需要，而对于高素质、复合型商务英语人才的需求已成为时代发展的必然趋势。"国际商务系列教材"（Series of International Business）就是在经济全球化成为现实，国与国之间相互依赖的时代而推出的。它联合了众多高等院校具有丰富教学实践经验的专家、教授编写而成。本系列教材对于国际商务专业的学生具有非常强的指导性和可操作性。

　　本系列教材旨在为人们提供系统和实用的国际商务知识、规范和原则，通过学习国际商务相关知识，提高自己的竞争能力，减少失误和误会，赢得更多的商机。本系列教材的编写力图做到时效性、全面性、创新性、生动性、准确性、实用性和客观性。在内容上尽可能做到与时俱进，贴近时代，并具有可操作性和可移植性。其内容丰富，选材广泛，深入浅出，编排紧凑，特别适用于国际商务专业硕士、商务英语方向研究生，商务英语本科生作为教材，也适用于业内人士自修和工作参考。

　　我们诚恳希望广大专家和师生给我们提出宝贵的意见和建议。

张立玉

2013 年春天

前　言

随着全球经济一体化趋势的日益发展，国际间的商务往来活动日益频繁，竞争越来越激烈，商务交往手段越来越新颖化、多样化，商务活动已经不再局限于卖出单向交流，而是由内向外——从公司内部的运营到商场的服务，从个人的专业知识、才能到言行举止，达到全方位的人际交流。随着近年来中国的政治和经济实力不断地提升，特别是中国加入世界贸易组织以来，中国经济以前所未有的深度和广度继续对外开放，日益融入到区域经济和全球经济一体化的框架中，人们需要学习更多的商务礼仪，遵守一些现代商务礼仪规范，熟悉中国商务礼仪，了解世界其他国家的礼仪和禁忌。

《国际商务礼仪》一书旨在为人们提供系统和实用的商务礼仪的规范、原则和技巧，通过学习商务基本礼仪规范，帮助读者及从业人员了解中国与西方国家的商务礼仪文化差异，从而提高交际能力。

全书共分 12 个章节，从商务接待、商务宴请、办公室礼仪、面试礼仪、社交礼仪、谈判礼仪、旅行礼仪、餐饮礼仪等方面，详细地阐述了跨文化交际中的基本礼仪常识。每个章节都有其独立的商务礼仪内容，突出介绍一些商务礼仪的基本原则和运作技巧，旨在为全球化生活、学习和工作环境中的交际者提供基本的行为指引，人们还可以通过学习国际商务礼仪规范，消除礼仪差异导致的交际障碍，提高交际的有效性，以便提高自己的竞争能力，减少职场的失误和误会，从而赢得更多的商机。

作者在著本书过程中，参考了国内外有关书籍和资料，个别地方引用了现成资料，在此特向原作者致以衷心的感谢！由于作者水平有限，不足之处在所难免，敬请读者批评指正。

张立玉

2014 年 10 月于武昌珞珈山

CONTENTS

目 录

Chapter 1

An Introduction of Business Etiquette

Etiquette has to do with good manners. It is not so much our own good manners, but making other people feels comfortable by the way we behave. It is more or less thinking of others and how others perceive us. An etiquette or good manner is one of those basic principles. Rules of good behavior have been built up over hundreds of years; worthless ones are continually being discarded and those proven to be useful are kept and improved upon.

≫ 1.1 The Definition of Etiquette

Etiquette refers to some standard behaviors observed by people in their communication. It is also a kind of civilization accumulation of home being and becomes fixed, handed down from generation to generation. Many experts say that etiquette is simply showing respect for others and yourself at the same time. So, even though aspects of good manners do vary from place to place and some rules may be added to keep up with technology or lifestyles — the foundation of etiquette, its meaning, will forever remain strong.

Good manners are not only indispensable in society, but they have a very practical value in the business world. Breeding is an essential part of the equipment of anyone who wishes to go far in his particular work or profession. No doubt many failures can be traced to *boorishness*(粗鲁), to lack of consideration for one's fellows, to neglect of the courtesies essential to civilized living... In both social and business life we seek the people with whom we can be at ease, the people whose manners do not offend us and in whose company we feel entirely comfortable. There is, indeed, nothing that costs less and at the same time is of more value to you than good manners... However, it must be remembered that... Just as words die from our language and others are born into it, just as skirts soar to the knees one season and tumble to the ankles the next, so do the formalities and outward gestures of etiquette vary according to the times. Although the spirit of etiquette remains always essentially the same, the expression of etiquette — the rules of conduct which govern social life and our associations with one another, is forever adjusting itself to new conditions. So, in other words, learn the definition of etiquette early. Take in all the basic knowledge that you can now, so that you too can adjust to our ever changing world.

≫ 1. 2   The Definition of Business Etiquette

Business etiquette is a kind of good manners performed by businessmen in their business activity. As good manners can guide them to behave in a certain way, the important element for a successful business is to acquire a good knowledge of different business etiquettes.

In recent years, business environment is becoming increasingly more global. Meetings, phone calls and conferences are held all over the world and attendees can come from any point on the globe. On any given business day, We can find ourselves dealing face-to-face, over the phone, by e-mail and, on rare occasions, by postal letter with people whose customs and cultures differ our own. We may never have to leave home to interact on an international level.

While the English old saying "When in Rome, do as the Romans do" still holds true, business clients and colleagues who are visiting this country should be treated with sensitivity and with an awareness of their unique culture. As we know every culture represents a certain choice of behavior patterns from the infinite patterns of human experiences. Not to do your homework and put your best international foot forward can cost you relationships and future business. One small misstep such as using first names inappropriately, not observing the rules of timing or sending the wrong color flower in the welcome bouquet can be costly.

≫ 1. 3   Rules of Business Etiquette

There is no one set of rules that applies to all international visitors so do the research for each country that our clients represent. That may sound like a daunting task, but taken in small steps, it is manageable and the rewards are worth the effort. Keeping in mind that there are as many ways to do business as there are countries to do business with, here are a few tips for minding your global P's and Q's.

1) Building Relationships

When we do business with foreign clients, it is advisable to take time to get to know our clients and build rapport before you rush to the bottom line. Business relationships are built on trust that is developed over time, especially with people from Asia and America.

2) Dressing Conservatively

People in some countries like to dress for fashion and comfort (e. g. American), but people from other parts of the world are generally more conservative. Our choice of business attire is a signal of our respect for the other person or organization. It is advisable to leave your trendy clothes in the closet on the days that you meet with our foreign guests.

3) Observe the Hierarchy

It is not always a simple matter to know who the highest-ranking member is when we are dealing with a group. To avoid embarrassment, err on the side of age and masculine gender, only if we are unable to discover the protocol with research. If we are interacting with the Japanese, it is important to understand that they make decisions by consensus, starting with the younger members of the group. By contrast, Latin people have a clear hierarchy that defers to age.

4) Understanding the Handshake

With a few exceptions, business people around the world use the handshake for meeting and greeting. However, the styles vary among different countries. For example, the American style handshake with a firm grip, two quick pumps, eye contact and a smile is not universal. Variations in handshakes are based on cultural differences, not on personality or values. The Japanese give a light handshake. Germans offer a firm shakes with one pump, and the French grip is light with a quick pump. Middle Eastern people will continue shaking your hand throughout the greeting. Don't be surprised if you are occasionally met with a kiss, a hug, or a bow somewhere along the way.

5) Using Title and Correct Forms of Address

People are very informal in the United States and are quick to call others by their first name. Approach first names with caution when dealing with people from other cultures. Use titles and last names until you have been invited to use the person's first name. In some cases, this may never occur. Use of first names is reserved for family and close friends in some cultures.

Titles are given more significance around the world than in the United States and are another important aspect of addressing business people. Earned academic degrees are acknowledged. For example, a German engineer is addressed as "Herr Ingenieur" and a professor as "Herr Professor". Listen carefully when you are introduced to someone and pay attention to business cards when you receive them.

6) Exchanging Business Cards

The key to giving out business cards in any culture is to show respect for the other person. Present your card so that the other person does not have to turn it over to read your information. Use both hands to present your card to visitors from Japan, China, Singapore. When you receive someone else's business card, always look at it and acknowledge it. When you put it away, place it carefully in your card case or with your business documents. Sticking it haphazardly in your pocket is demeaning to the giver. In most cases, wait until you have been introduced to give someone your card.

7) Valuing Time

Not everyone in the world is as time conscious as Americans. Don't take it personally if someone from a more relaxed culture keeps you waiting or spends more of that commodity than you normally would in meetings or over meals. Stick to the rules of punctuality, but understand when your contact from another country seems unconcerned.

8) Honoring Space Issues

In general, people in a country have a particular value for their own physical space and are uncomfortable when other people get in their realm. If the foreign visitors seem to want to be close, accept it. Backing away can send the wrong message. So can touching. You shouldn't risk violating someone else's space by touching them in any way other than with a handshake.

Whether the world comes to you or you go out to it, the greatest compliment you can pay your international clients is to learn about their country and their customs. Understand differences in behavior and honor them with your actions. Don't take offense when visitors behave according to their norms. People from other cultures will appreciate your efforts to accommodate them and you will find yourself building your international clientele.

⋙ 1.4　Business Etiquettes in China

Doing business in one country could be quite different from the way in which it is done in another country. Doing business in China means that business people will come into increasingly frequent contact with Chinese business people and officials. It is imperative that those doing business in China learn about areas such business culture, business etiquette, meeting protocol and negotiation techniques in order to maximize the potential of their business trip. Here are some business etiquettes in China:

1) Greetings

When businessmen do business with people from the other cultures, it is avoidable to make a greetings or introduction, which is the very important in business activities. Address a person using his or her family name only, such as Mr. Chen or Ms. Hsu. The Chinese family name comes first and is usually one syllable. A one or a two-syllable given name follows a family name. For example, in the case of Zheng Linyin, Zheng is the family name and Linyin is the given name. In some instances, Westernized Chinese might reverse their names when visiting and sending correspondence abroad. Therefore, it is always a good idea to ask a native speaker which name is the family name.

For business purposes, it is traditionally acceptable to call a Chinese person by the surname, together with a title, such as "Director Wang" or "Chairman Li. " Avoid using someone's given name unless you have known him or her for a long period of time. Formality is a sign of respect, and it is advisable to clarify how you will address someone very early in a relationship, generally during your first meeting.

Do not try to become too friendly too soon, and do not insist that your Chinese counterparts address you by your given name. The Western pattern of quick informality should be resisted.

Chinese way of greeting is a nod or slight bow. However, when interacting with Westerners, Chinese usually shake hands. Bear in mind that a soft handshake and a lack of eye contact do not necessarily indicate timidity. It only implies that the person is not accustomed to the firm handshakes commonly used in the West.

2) Business Meetings

In China, it is assumed that the first person that enters the room is the head of the group. Westerners should observe this convention so as not to confuse the Chinese. Important guests are usually escorted to their seats. If the meeting room has a large central table, the principal guest is likely to be seated directly opposite the principal host.

When you exchange business cards, hold out your card using both hands with the writing facing the recipient. Cards should always be exchanged individually (one-on-one). Never toss or "deal" your business card across the table, as this is considered extremely rude. Receive a business card with both hands and scan it immediately for vital information. Then lay the card in front of you on the table. It is demeaning to put someone's card directly into your pocket without looking at it first.

Meetings begin with small talk. Resist the temptation to get down to business right away. Also, avoid telling western-style jokes, because jokes sometimes do not translate across cultures and can cause confusion or hurt feelings.

3) Social Events

In social events, seating arrangement is often determined by the host, being a guest, you should wait to be seated rather than seating themselves. At a formal banquet, do not eat or drink anything (except tea) until the host/hostess has delivered the welcome toast and eating.

If you are the guest of honor, be prepared to give a short, friendly speech in response to the host's speech. It is polite to sample every dish served. Your host may serve some food for you, and it is nice to reciprocate if you feel comfortable doing so.

Never drink your alcoholic drink alone. If you would like to take a sip from it, find someone else at the table that you can toast with and them you can drink.

The Chinese hosts often place some food on their guests' plates as a sign of respect, do not feel obliged to finish everything on your plate, just leave something on your plate at the end of the meal or your host might think that you are still hungry.

No matter how good a drinker you are, do not challenge a Chinese into a drinking contest. As big drinkers, certainty they will win.

4) Gift-giving

Unlike many countries, the giving of gifts does not carry any negative connotations when doing business in China. Gifts should always be exchanged for celebrations, as thanks for assistance and even as a sweetener for future favors. However, it is important not to give gifts in the absence of a good reason or a witness. This may be construed differently.

When the Chinese want to buy gifts it is not uncommon for them to ask what you would like. Do not be shy to specify something you desire. However, it would be wise to demonstrate an appreciation of Chinese culture by asking for items such as ink paintings or tea. Business gifts are always reciprocated. They are seen as debts that must be repaid.

When you give gifts, do not give cash. They need to be items of worth or beauty. Do not be too frugal with your choice of gift otherwise you will be seen as an "iron rooster", i. e. , getting a good gift out of you is like getting a feather out of an iron rooster.

If is appropriate to bring a gift, particularly something representative of your town or region, to a business meeting or social event. Gifts indicate that you are interested in building a relationship. A gift should always be wrapped, but avoid plain black or white paper because these are the colors of mourning. Present the gift with both hands as a sign of courtesy and always mention that this is only a small token of appreciation. Do not expect your gift to be opened in your presence. This indicates that it is the thought that counts more than the material value.

Never give a clock, handkerchief, umbrella or white flowers, specifically chrysanthemums, as a gift, as all of these signify tears and/or death. Never give sharp objects such as knives or scissors as they would signify the cutting of a relationship. Lucky numbers are 6 and 8 (especially in a series, such as 66 or 888). An unlucky number is 4.

≫ 1. 5   The Important Role of Business Etiquette

Business etiquette plays a very important role in foreign business. Companies know that business etiquette skills can directly affect productivity, profits and retention. Doing business with foreign clients requires more than just financial acumen. A lack of knowledge about a customer's culture can lead to misunderstanding, frustration and potential embarrassment. When making market research, exporters should have a clear picture of their foreign clients' cultures and regional etiquettes when preparing to export. The building of successful business relationships is a vital part of any international venture, and such relationships rely heavily on an understanding of each partner's expectations and intentions.

Each culture has its own *idiosyncrasies* when it comes to social business relations. As a representative of your company, you want to ensure that you make the best impression on potential clients — and that means having at least a basic familiarity with the customs and practices of the region.

When you discuss business with your customers, you may not pay attention to your behavior and that business etiquette plays an important role during business communications. Your success depends not only on what you say, but how you say it.

≫ 1. 6   Some Tips

1) Meeting Etiquette

Here is a correct way to greet people in a formal manner:

- Providing a good, firm handshake is a great start to making a good business relationship.
- For men, when making presentations or meeting with important clients, you should dress in a conservatively cut business suit. You should wear a long sleeved shirt and a smartly patterned tie, both of which should coordinate with the suit. Shoes should be of a dark color and polished, and accompanied by a belt of a matching color.
- For women, in more formal business situations, should dress in a conservative suit or a well tailored dress accompanied by a jacket. She should also wear stockings and a closed toe pump or dress shoes for footwear. It is wise for the heel not to exceed one and a half inches.
- Makeup and accessories should tastefully coordinate with the rest of the outfit.
- Looking businesslike is the first step to acting businesslike, and people will take you more seriously if you are well-groomed. This also applies to body language, so always make eye contact and keep good posture, or you may appear to lack confidence.
- There is one more thing that you should remember. Remember people's names and they will remember you. Do everything you can to avoid addressing a message "Dear Sir/Madam". Remember that business is about building relationships.
- Do learn a few words of foreign language. This shows an interest in your host's language and culture. It also is a very good icebreaker.

2) Greetings & Introduction

We exchange greetings with people almost every day. Therefore, English for greetings is of primary importance in oral English practice. A good command of it can make you polite and sociable.

When we talk with a stranger, we usually use Sir when he is a man and Miss or Madam for a woman. If we happen to know the surname of the person we are talking to, we use Mr. in front of the surname for a man, Mrs. for a married woman and Miss for a single woman. If you are familiar with each other, you may address him or her by the first name to show your friendship. Most Europeans' names have three parts. For example, David Herbert Lawrence. David is the first name or given name. Herbert is the Christian name and Lawrence is the family or surname or the last name.

When meeting somebody the first time, it is polite to introduce yourself first. You can ask somebody's name, home country, hometown, etc. , but you should not ask questions about age, living habit, address, and phone numbers, when talking to somebody of opposite sex. Those questions are too personal and would be viewed impolite. There are some questions you should never ask, no matter how long you have known him/her, such as a person's salary, property, financial situations and social security number.

If you want to know where a person was born, you can ask "Where are you originally from?" This way, you can avoid confusion, because people may have lived in different areas or countries, so "Where are you from?" can be confusing.

≫ **1. 7   Skills and Strategies**

1) Personal introduction

(1) If you have a minute, I'd like to introduce you a good friend of mine.
(2) Mr. Smith is one of our foremost clients and will be visiting our factory this afternoon.
(3) Mr. Li, I would like to introduce you Julia Green, our director in charge of marketing and distribution.
(4) If you have any questions about anything you see, or if you have any special requirements or needs, she can help to accommodate you.
(5) I am pleased to present our foremost customer, Ms. Mary Friend, who will be attending our meetings throughout the day.

2) Small Talks

(1) Hi there, I'm Steve Saunders.
(2) Is this the first conference you've been to?
(3) Yes, it is, better than I expected it would be.
(4) Have you been here for a long time?
(5) It's a great job, I can spend a lot of my time outdoors, and I also get to ski for free all seasons.

3) Congratulations and best wishes

(1) It's great to hear about your promotion.

(2) Congratulations on your success!

(3) I'd like to be the first to congratulate you.

(4) Every success in your business.

(5) May you success in your business.

(6) Congratulations on landing that contract.

(7) Congratulations on that deal.

(8) This is really a good deal. May I congratulate you?

4) Expressing praise and thanks

(1) Your knowledge of Chinese is really surprising.

(2) I've been admiring your cuff links.

(3) I really love your hairstyle, it looks quite elegant.

(4) I do appreciate your timely help.

(5) I really don't know how I can thank you enough.

(6) You are the most capable person I've ever seen.

(7) I can't thank you enough for your understanding and cooperation.

(8) You really have an eye for beauty.

5) Expressing likes and dislikes

(1) Stamp-collecting is a lovely way to pass the time.

(2) I'm much on aerobic activity.

(3) There is nothingI enjoy more than going to the pictures.

(4) I'm not over-enthusiastic about surf-riding.

(5) I especially dislike fatty meat.

(6) The lyrics are rubbish.

(7) I'm afraid I don't like taking buses.

(8) I'm crazy about the subtropical island.

Chapter 2

Business Etiquette in Reception

Different countries have different cultural traditions; as a result, their business etiquette in reception also varies from one another. We all know it is not easy to imagine that when we are in mixed company in social situations for the purpose of conducting business that a myriad of situations can unexpectedly arise. Therefore, knowing what is expected in these types of situations helps us anticipate potential problems and maintain our professional image as we muddle through.

>>> 2.1 The Definition of Business Etiquette in Reception

Business etiquette in reception refers to a kind of standard behavior observed by the businessmen in their communication with their business partners. As it is involved in common business activities such as making appointment, communicating with business partners, writing and giving welcome or farewell speeches, etc., it is a very important part in building relationship with business partners and it can influence their success or failure. Thus it is in essence a way of maximizing their business potential.

In business circle, reception is the first point of contact with your partners, as it can make an impression on external stakeholders such as customers and investors. Such being a case, a businessman must abide by an etiquette that meets the company's standards.

Before meeting your new foreign business partners, it is advisable to know all appointments and whereabouts of the executives. Only in this way can you receive and talk to them without any hesitancy. It is also very important to know the visitor's name, title and company he/she represents, and the purpose of his/her visit. When receiving visitors, you should receive them properly; make them feel comfortable and know how to deal with them professionally. For example, making guests feel welcome and greet greeting them at once on heir entering the reception area. When the visitors leave, you should walk them to the front door, and thank him for coming and say goodbye.

≫ 2.2   Some Basic Rules for Reception Etiquette

There are some general guidelines for some common "mixing business and pleasure" scenarios:

1) Note that "cocktail reception" on an invitation typically refers to a "business appropriate" style of dress as well as light/appetizer food and beverage. However, it does not always, as some people incorrectly assume indicate informal, free liquor to all, bring along two friends and get drunk party. Professionals with business on their mind will dress as if they were going to work, bring along their business cards, and have something to eat before they go, leave their college buddies at home and refrain from drinking too much.

2) Conversations about children and family do have their place in "networking" situations for business. Small talk can be a very effective icebreaker. Just be mindful of getting too personal and speak about your own personal experiences — don't pass on personal or familial information about coworkers or clients. Try not to dwell on the subject either. After a couple of polite questions or comments, move on the next topic.

3) At conventions, it is absolutely necessary to participate or at least make an appearance at most organized functions. If your travel expenses and accommodations are on the company expense account, remember that business is your priority. Chances are you'll be expected to bring home some new ideas and contact information.

4) People are more likely to remember your name if they see it, hear it and say it, all within a few seconds. This is primarily why it's good to wear your nametag on the right hand side, carry business cards with you at all times and make a point of practicing a self introduction. Say your name clearly and add a couple of clever lines that instigate interest and draw questions from others.

5) You need not always take a drink if offered one in a "mixing" situation. Sometimes people feel obligated to do so thinking it will make others who are drinking feel comfortable. If you don't drink or don't feel like drinking, simply decline graciously but resist making comment as to why you don't drink or whether or not you approve of them drinking. If you're the hostess, don't insist that someone else drink and don't over serve.

6) If you have to make a quick exit to attend another function, you should make an effort to say goodbye to the host and thank them. It is not generally necessary to explain why you are departing early particularly if you're off to attend another function.

7) It is not necessary to eat at a "mixing" function where food just to give others the impression that you are comfortable and at ease. Some people are just not relaxed unless they have something to do with their hands so they eat thinking it will help them appear less nervous. Chances are you will not be approached often if your hands are full of BBQ sauce or your

mouth is full of cheese ball. Remember that most everyone is nervous in a room full of strangers so take a deep breath and use your hands for handshaking rather than eating.

8) In mixing situations, men and women should interact with each other the same way they would in social situations. Never forget that when it comes to modern business, gender is not an issue. Rank is the only thing that matters. If you would extend courtesies such as offering to get drinks or hang coats or hold doors to women, also extend these courtesies to men.

9) If you are invited to a "social" function with business associates, it is not OK to bring along a friend or spouse unless the hostess or the invitation specifically states that you may do so. If you are uncomfortable attending alone, call the hostess in advance and ask that they meet you at the door and introduce you to a couple of people or seat you with someone else who is coming alone. Whatever you do, do not bring along your best buddy for comfort and then hang out together by the shrimp tree all night long.

10) When invited to company "social" functions like baseball games, picnics, family events, etc. , it is not acceptable to bring along business cards and talk business. Usually these types of "mixing" functions are for the purpose of making extended family and associates feel welcome and build social relationships between coworkers and/or clients. Save the business lingo and work oriented conversations for Monday at the office.

≫ 2. 3   The Basic Steps in Receiving Business Partners

When we receive foreign business partners, it is advisable to follow the basic steps in receiving the guests, which listed below:

1) Know where accessible restrooms, drinking fountains and telephones are located. If such facilities are not available, be ready to offer alternatives, such as the private or employee restroom, a glass of water or your desk phone.

2) When extending a verbal welcome, try to use a normal tone of voice; do not raise your voice unless requested.

3) When introduced to a person with a disability, it is appropriate to offer to shake hands. People with limited hand use or who wear an artificial limb can usually shake hands.

4) Shaking hands with the left hand is acceptable.

5) For those who cannot shake hands, touch the person on the shoulder or arm to welcome and acknowledge their presence.

6) Treat adults in a manner befitting adults.

7) Call a person by his or her first name only when extending that familiarity to all others present.

8) Never patronize people using wheelchairs by patting them on the head or shoulder.

9) When addressing a person who uses a wheelchair, never lean on the person's wheelchair. The chair is part of the space that belongs to the person who uses it.

10) When talking with a person with a disability, look at and speak directly to that person rather than through a companion who may be along.

11) If an interpreter is present, speak to the person who has scheduled the appointment, not to the interpreter. Always maintain eye contact with the applicant, not the interpreter.

12) Offer assistance in a dignified manner with sensitivity and respect. Be prepared to have the offer declined. Do not proceed to assist if your offer to assist is declined. If the offer is accepted, listen to or accept instructions.

13) Allow a person with a visual impairment to take your arm (at or about the elbow.) This will enable you to guide rather than propel or lead the person.

14) Offer to hold or carry packages in a welcoming manner.

Example: *May I help you with your packages?*

15) When offering to hand a coat or umbrella, do not offer to hand a cane or crutches unless the individual requests otherwise.

≫ 2. 4   The Functions of Business Reception

Business reception involves a variety of administrative support functions, such as scheduling appointments, answering the phone, greeting visitors and making sure the reception area is tidy and welcoming. Reception work is very important as it can affect the success of the company.

Excellent telephone etiquette comes first in reception, because a large portion of business activities relates to answering, screening and transferring phone calls. Being a receptionist, he/she should speak slowly and clearly, and should not have food, beverages or gum in his/her mouth.

When receiving the visitors, a receptionist should follow proper communication etiquette. No matter he/she is on the phone or greeting visitors in person, he/she should be patient with the visitors, even if visitors express frustration or anger, he/she must remain calm and patient at all times.

In business, professional etiquette can create a positive impression of the company. And reception is the first front of the business. As a result, executives often want their employees to demonstrate proper professional etiquette. Being a receptionist, he/she is the first person to greet visitors as they come through the door, he/she should wear standard business attire and be well groomed.

Furthermore, a professional reception area is very important, it entails maintaining an environment that is clean, comfortable and welcoming for the visitors. You should keep things neat and clean, provide magazines for the visitors to read while they wait, offer visitors coffee or water, and greet visitors appropriately. The receptionists are the liaisons between the clients and the business, for they are the first person that the visitors see and speak to during their visit or call. The interaction that the visitors have with the receptionist can make or break the overall business relationship.

Besides, appearance and body language is also part of good etiquette in reception. You should maintain clean hair, nail and skin. Your clothing should be fresh, matching and wrinkle free and your body language should show you are interested in your position, your company and your partners. When a guest arrives, sit up straight and make eye contact with that person, then smile and offer the guest a seat or a beverage. In a word, your overall appearance should be welcoming to him/her, he/she should feel comfortable and confident that he/she has the made the right business choice.

≫≫ 2.5　The Responsibility in Reception

The responsibilities in business reception may differ from one company to another, but common responsibilities concern about directing telephone calls, providing information about the company, and bookkeeping.

As a receptionist, he/she takes the responsibility of directing incoming calls from customers, clients and employees. He/she should answer these calls, transfer them to the appropriate employees, forward messages and answer general questions.

As visitors and employees enter an office, in general, the first employee they usually encounter is the receptionist. A receptionist ensures each visitors is greeted and that proper identification is shown in cases where building access is limited to specific individuals. He/she should also hand out visitor passes, inform employees of arriving guests, direct guests to their destinations and make sure the security department is at once notified of unauthorized visitors.

Another responsibility that a receptionist should take is to assist other administrative staff, he/she should expect to perform data entry, word processing, assist with setting up conference rooms and handle other light clerical work when asked.

A receptionist is also required to schedule future appointments and notify the appropriate personnel of cancellations. He/she may ensure outgoing mail is sent and that incoming mail is distributed to the appropriate recipients. It is necessary for him or her to accept and distributing the morning paper to the appropriate personnel, sign for packages and updating office directory information.

⟫ 2.6　Some Tips for Business Reception

1) Think Before You Speak

In talking to a person you have just met and about whom you know nothing, the best approach is to try one topic after another, usually not by asking questions that can be answered "yes" or "no" but by asking his advice or opinion. From his answer, hopefully you can carry on a conversation. Don't be afraid of a period of silence and chatter about anything at all just to fill it. Think before you speak. Dorothy Sarnoff wrote: "*I* is the smallest letter in the alphabet. Don't make it the largest word in your vocabulary. Say, with Socrates, not ' I think, ' but what do you think?" you will leave the person with the impression that you are an interesting and interested person and, just as important, a good listener when you don't monopolize the conversation out of panic that nothing will be said if you don't carry the conversational ball all by yourself. Of course, take your turn, describing something you have been doing or an interesting article you have read, then stop and ask your new acquaintance his opinion about or experiences with the topic.

When you want to end a conversation, it is up to you to find acceptable structures. Often these can include a hint for your leaving or a reason for having to leave (like "Nice talking to you" or "Sorry, I must get back to work", etc.). It is usual practice to end a conversation politely. Just walking away would be considered extremely rude.

2) Receiving Business Partners

When the business partner is from nearly, and you just want to leave the office you merely say quite frankly, "I'm terribly sorry, but we were just leaving for... Could you come back another time?" But make the future date right then and there. "Another time" left at that means little, but a firm invitation proves that you would really enjoy a visit at a more convenient time. If your earlier plans were such that they could be carried out on another day, it would of course be more polite to postpone them and stay at office with your visitor.

If you are just about to start your dinner when business partners drop in, you must try to make the meal stretch to include them. If they say, "Oh, no, thank you — we've just eaten, " then pull up a chair for them, offer them a cup of coffee or a cold drink, and ask their forgiveness while you finish your meal.

3) Case Study

A. Read the customer satisfactory form. Which three of the criteria are most important to you?

The Moon River Restaurant

Thank you for choosing to eat at The Moon River Restaurant. We are constantly striving to improve the quality of our service and would welcome your comments. Please help us by taking a few moments to complete this form

	Excellent	Satisfactory	Poor
Atmosphere	☐	☐	☐
Clearness	☐	☐	☐
Location	☐	☐	☐
Comfort	☐	☐	☐
Speed of Service	☐	☐	☐
Value for Money	☐	☐	☐
Staff Friendliness	☐	☐	☐
Staff Attentiveness	☐	☐	☐
Quality of Drink	☐	☐	☐
Quality of Food	☐	☐	☐

We look forward to your next visit.

The Moon River Restaurant, 42 Butts Road, Oxford,

OX3 2JR UK   Tel: 0186—544836

B. Read the profile of the business people below. Choose ways of entertaining them from the following list.

- a shopping trip
- a sightseeing tour of the city
- a visit to a sports event
- a round of golf
- a meal at an expensive restaurant

1. Tom Peterson, 32, the Sales Manager of a British computer software company. This is a new but important customer. He has a two-day stopover on his way to London.

2. A party of five Japanese businessmen in their mid-thirties. They are finding mission to help them decide whether to offer your company a substantial contract.

3. Frida Mellor, 46, the Managing Director of your company's largest client. He is flying in from Milan to finalize one or two small details concerning a major deal with you. His wife, Andrea,

is with him on his trip.

4. Angela Goddard, 36, the Manager of Shirts & Shofrts, a manufacturer of fashion sportswear, and her personal assistant, Andrea Meier. Several orders you placed with their company arrived late. As a result, you nearly lost a valued customer.

≫ **2.7 Skills and Strategies**

1) Greeting visitors

(1) Please come in.

(2) This way, please.

(3) Please sit down.

(4) Please make yourself at home.

(5) Please help yourself.

(6) Just a moment.

(7) MayI have your name, please?

2) Expressing your rejection

(1) No more, thank you.

(2) Not for me, thank you.

(3) I'm sorry, but I won't be able to come.

(4) Let's make it some other time.

(5) I have a previous engagement.

3) Asking someone to wait

(1) Wait!

(2) Wait a minute!

(3) Wait it out!

(4) Just one moment!

(5) I'll be back in just a second!

(6) Wait your turn.

(7) Hold your horses.

4) Receiving clients

(1) Would you like me to show you around while you are waiting?

(2) I was wondering if I could speak to someone about investment accounts with your company.

(3) Let me find out if he made arrangements for someone else to meet with you in his place.

(4) Go ahead and have a seat, make yourself comfortable.

(5) It's a busy time for us right now, but if you don't mind waiting about ten minutes, I can arrange for you to talk with Mr. Smith.

5) Entertaining clients

(1) I'd be happy to take you around this city and show you the sights tonight if you're up to it.

(2) How does that schedule sound to you?

(3) I've already made a hotel reservation for you, let's go to the hotel first and drop off your things.

(4) I'd like to have a drink so that we can get better acquainted, I've booked a table at an exclusive restaurant downtown.

(5) Over the next few days, if you have any questions or problems, I will be right here to help you.

7) Factory tours

(1) I'll be showing you around today.

(2) Here, let's move on to the next room.

(3) We'd like to welcome everyone to BY Tools factory site, and thank everyone for being here.

(4) To maintain a level of safety, we also require all of our staff to wear protective gear.

(5) Here in the main plant is where most of the action takes place.

(6) We have about 40 employees on the ground floor, which is about 20% of the total staff.

(7) I'd like to show you what it looks like in one of our test cubicles.

(8) We produce and package more than ten hundred thousand units per year onthese machines.... if you do the math on it that breaks down to about one unit every minute.

8) Accommodating foreign clients

(1) I will be able to go along with you.

(2) I can be your interpreter and tour guide.

(3) Over the next few days, if you have any questions or problems, I will be right here to help you out.

(4) My pleasure, I hope your visit to China is very enjoyable.

(5) If you don't mind, we'd like to invite you to dinner.

(6) Let me show you, this is how it works, the chopsticks become extensions of your fingers, just hold them like this, and grab the food by pinching the two chopsticks together with your hand.

Chapter 3

Business Etiquette in Office

An office is a place where many meetings happen every day. Because of this, an effective office manager will publish current conference room schedules and make them available to her staff. He/She also needs to be able to manage her staffing and provide for adequate coverage when employees are on personal leave. In order to make an office run efficiently, office etiquette plays an important part. An office manager has a good command of the skills necessary for successful office management organizational skills including proper office etiquette.

⟫ 3.1   The Definition of Office Etiquette

As we know different situations require different types of etiquette. Office etiquette refers to a code of behavior that delineates expectations for social behavior according to contemporary conventional norms within a society, social class, or a group. To put it simple, office etiquette is the conventional requirements of social behavior; it refers to observing a simple set of rules for getting along with others and conducting yourself respectfully and courteously in the office or workplace.

Office etiquette covers the proper ways of using your cell phone, telephone, e-mail and twitter at work, proper behaviors at office parties and business meals, wearing appropriate office attire, etc.

Good office etiquette can be easily achieved by using common courtesy as a matter of course, as the essence of good manners is to be respectful and courteous at all times and with everybody. Therefore, treat your coworkers and business partners with respect and courtesy.

⟫ 3.2   Office Party Etiquette

Are you planning to attend an office party? An office party gives you the opportunity to celebrate the holidays or other occasion with your coworkers. You should have fun, but be careful about having too good a time. Here are "ten office party don'ts". Avoiding them can save your professional reputation.

1) Don't Drink too Much

Alcohol lowers your inhibitions and alters your judgment. It can make you do things you may regret. Even if you think you can handle your alcohol quite well, one mixed drink or a glass of wine at the office party should be your limit. Remember, perception is everything. You don't want to look like you're drinking too much, even if alcohol has little effect on you.

2) Don't Treat the Office Party like a Singles Bar

An office party gives you a chance to see another side of your coworkers. However, you shouldn't try to get to know any of them *too well*. Jim (or Jane) from accounting may suddenly look a lot more appealing under bar lights than cubicle lights. Ignore your animal instincts. Workplace romances — or worse, one night stands — can be disastrous.

3) Don't Flirt or Act in a Sexually Provocative Manner

Your flirting may be entirely innocent, but the message it sends to your colleagues isn't innocent. If you want to be respected on a professional level, you should save this side of yourself for parties with friends.

4) Don't Wear Suggestive Clothing

If you wouldn't wear it to the office, you shouldn't wear it to the office party. Of course, your clothes can be more festive than those you wear to work (think sequins, color, and sparkles), but they shouldn't be revealing.

5) Don't Let Your Guard Down (forget to be careful)

People tend to relax at office parties. When relaxed, we let our guards down and reveal things about ourselves we don't want our co-workers to know. Alcohol may contribute to this too, so be sure to pay careful attention to item.

6) Don't Tell Dirty or Off-Color Jokes

This rule holds true in or out of the office. Dirty or off-color jokes may be offensive to others, so avoid telling them.

7) Don't Use Foul Language

You may feel so comfortable at the office party that you forget you're really at work. Keep bad language in check as it could make you look unprofessional.

8) Don't Talk About People Behind Their Backs

Just because someone is absent from the office party it doesn't give you reason to talk about him behind his back. In addition to the fact that it's just not nice, this person's friends may be present and word could get back to him.

9) Don't Bring Uninvited Guests

Often office parties are for employees only. Don't assume it's OK to bring your significant other or someone else without asking first.

10) Don't Underestimate the Importance of Your Guest's Behavior

If it's OK to bring a guest, choose wisely. Invite someone who will behave appropriately. That means he or she will have to follow the same rules you are expected to follow.

≫ 3. 3   Cell Phone Etiquette

There comes a time in any technological revolution when some basic guidelines need to be laid down. It happened when e-mail exploded on the scene and people started to learn some basic dos's and don'ts around the new medium. For example, if you copy the boss in on an e-mail message to a colleague, it means that you are through kidding around. No one teaches these things in company training; they are just things that get learned.

In terms of cell phone use, there are some real abuses of wireless technology being perpetrated all around us, and the time has come to create some social order out of the cell phone chaos. This is by no means an exhaustive list simply because as the technology evolves, new annoying traits will surely emerge. If you bring your cell phone to work, here are some rules of etiquette you should follow to make sure you don't offend your coworkers and your boss, and possibly jeopardize your job.

1) Do Not Subject Defenseless Others to Cell Phone Conversations

When people cannot escape the banality of your conversation, such as on the bus, in a cab, on a grounded airplane, or at the dinner table, you should spare them. People around you should have the option of not listening. If they don't, you shouldn't be babbling.

2) Do Not Set the Ringer to Play Beethoven's Fifth Every Time the Phone Rings

Or any other annoying melody. Is it not enough that phones go off every other second? Now we have to listen to synthesized nonsense.

3) Turn the Cell Phone off During Public Performances

We are not even sure this one needs to be said, but given the repeated violations of this heretofore unwritten law, we felt compelled to include it.

4) Do Not Wear More than Two Wireless Devices on the Belt

This has not become a big problem yet. But with plenty of techno-jockeys sporting pagers and phones, Batman-esque utility belts are sure to follow. Let's nip this one in the bud.

5) Do Not Dial While Driving

In all seriousness, this madness has to stop. There are enough people in the world who have problems mastering vehicles and phones individually. Put them together and we have a serious health hazard on our hands.

6) Do Not Wear the Earpiece When You Are Not on the Phone

This is not unlike being on the phone and carrying on another conversation with someone who is physically in your presence. No one knows if you are here or there. Very disturbing.

7) Do Not Speak Louder on the Cell Phone than You Would on Any Other Phone

These things have incredibly sensitive microphones, and it's gotten to the point where I can tell if someone is calling me from a cell because of the way they are talking, not how it sounds. If your signal cuts out, speaking louder won't help, unless the person is actually within earshot.

8) Do Not Grow too Attached to the Cell Phone

For obvious reasons, a dependency on constant communication is not healthy. At work, go nuts. At home, give it a rest.

9) Do Not Attempt to Impress with the Cell Phone

Not only is using a cell phone no longer impressive in any way, unless it's one of those really cool new phones with the space age design.

10) Do Not Slam the Cell Phone down on a Restaurant Table Just in Case It Rings

This is not the Old West, and you are not a gunslinger sitting down to a game of poker in the saloon. Could you please be a little less conspicuous? If it rings, you'll hear it just as well if it's in your coat pocket or clipped on your belt.

≫ 3. 4   E-mail Etiquette

Of all Internet activities, e-mail is the most popular. Almost 88 percent of all Internet users in the world use e-mail. According to the survey, approximately 90 percent of those who use the Internet at work use it to access business e-mail.

There is a good chance for one to use e-mail to communicate with others, including your boss, colleagues, clients, or prospective employers. You may find a lot of e-mail is well written. A lot of it isn't. Some messages go on and on and on, until finally the question is asked. Sometimes the length is necessary — other times the writer could be more concise.

Some messages get right to the point ... a little too quickly. The writer wastes no time asking for what he or she needs without bothering to be polite. Some people often use some sort of shorthand, i. e., "Can U plz send info on careers?" This may be appropriate for communicating with your buddies through instant messaging, but not for writing to someone you've never met. Besides, being a little more specific might help you find the information faster.

Sometimes there are glaring errors, such as misspellings and very poor grammar. We can only imagine what a prospective employer would think when receiving a poorly written message. Because your correspondence says a lot about you, you should be aware of some basic e-mail etiquette, sometimes known as etiquette.

1) Manners and Tone

What three words have a total of only 14 letters yet carry a great deal of meaning? People may not notice these words when they're there, but if you forget to use them, you'll come across looking disrespectful and ungrateful. Give up? These very powerful words are "*Please*", "*Thank You*", and "*Please take my advice*".

This isn't something that especially bothers one, but there are others who are very sensitive to being addressed by their first names. When in doubt, use Mr. , Mrs. , or Dr. (if appropriate). When you are replying to an e-mail and the sender of the original message has used his or her first name only, then you could safely assume it is OK to use that person's first name as well.

Tone is a difficult thing to explain. Remember when your parents would say "Don't use that tone of voice with me, young lady (or young man)?" Your feelings come across by the way you say something. It is easy to change your tone when you're speaking. When you're writing it's very hard to do. Whenever you write an e-mail, you need read your message over several times before you hit send. If you don't want to sound curt or demanding, you should make sure that you come across as respectful, friendly, and approachable. Sometimes just rearranging your paragraphs will help.

If you're writing to someone you've communicated with before, you might want to begin by saying "I hope you are well". E-mail writers often use emoticons to convey a certain tone. For those of you who don't know what these are, emoticons are little faces made up by arranging parentheses, colons, and semi-colons. Use good judgment here. If you write to someone frequently and you have a less formal relationship, then emoticons are OK. If, however, you're writing to a prospective employer, stick to words only.

Avoid writing your message using all uppercase letters. It looks like you're shouting. Don't use all 0 letters either. Some people say it will make it seem like you're mumbling.

2) Be Concise and Be Professional

When possible, be brief. Get to your point as quickly as you can. However, please don't leave out necessary details. If providing a lot of background information will help the recipient answer your query, by all means, include it. You may even want to apologize for being so wordy at the beginning of the message.

Young people often use all sorts of abbreviations — *U* instead of *you*, 2 instead of *to*, or *two*, *too*, *plz* instead of *please*, and *thanx* instead of *thanks*. It's fine for personal e-mail. Business e-mail should be more formal. Of course, frequently used abbreviations such as Mr. and Mrs. , FYI (for your information), inc. , etc. , are fine.

Take a look at your e-mail address. What does it say about you? Are you a sexymom@ isp. com? But do you want a prospective employer to think so? Think of getting a more formal address. Perhaps your first initial and last name would be good. If you're really attached to your address and don't want to change it, consider adding a second one for professional use only. If you're currently working, you may have a company e-mail account. Do not use this address for job hunting purposes. Use a personal account only.

3) Make a Good First Impression

E-mail is much less intrusive than a phone call and faster than a letter. It may be your introduction to someone you never met before. Take your time putting together a well-written message. Once you hit the send button you won't have another chance.

While a lot of people understand the importance of following certain rules when writing a business letter, they often forget these rules when composing an e-mail message. Just in case you've forgotten, letus refresh your memory.

a. Mind Your Manners

Think of the basic rules you learned growing up, like saying please and thank you. Address people you don't know as Mr. , Mrs. , or Dr. Only address someone by first name if they imply it's OK to do so.

b. Watch Your Tone

Merriam-Webster defines tone as an "accent or inflection expressive of a mood or emotion". It is very difficult to express tone in writing.

You want to come across as respectful, friendly, and approachable. You don't want to sound curt or demanding.

c. Be Concise

Get to the point of your e-mail as quickly as possible, but don't leave out important details that will help your recipient answer your query.

d. Be Professional

This means, stay away from abbreviations and don't use emoticons (those little smiley faces). Don't use a cute or suggestive e-mail address for business communications.

e. Use Correct Spelling and Proper Grammar

Use a dictionary or a spell checker — whichever works better for you. While you can write in a conversational tone (contractions are okay), pay attention to basic rules of grammar.

≫ 3.5 Office Communication Etiquette

As your company's representative, your phone manners should be impeccable. Too many workers who are abrupt on the phone rationalize their behavior by saying it is OK or even expected. Since they're at work, but this isn't true. You are putting across your company's image and should work just as hard at it on the phone as you would in person.

There are several accepted ways to answer a telephone at work. You can simply say "Hello" or you can say your name, as in "June Johnson speaking". You don't need to say the company's name if a receptionist or a secretary has already done so. Try to speak in a pleasant, unrushed voice. If you are rushed and can't talk, it's better to say this and make plans to call back later. Don't rustle papers or work while you're speaking on the phone. If you're really too distracted to speak, then reschedule the call.

It's OK and sometimes even necessary to screen your calls. But there's a right and a wrong way to do this. First, train your secretary to do it politely. It's better to ask " May I know who's calling?" than " Who is this?" or even " Who's calling?" Second, don't instruct your secretary to say you are out when you are in. It's acceptable to be in but too busy to talk at the moment and it's always better to be honest. Callers sense the difference, and besides, it may not look good if you're always out.

It's rude not to return telephone calls regardless of whom they are from. You might be ignoring a potential customer. Many people today don't bother to return phone calls, and if you work for someone else, it's highly unlikely that such behavior is acceptable. When you do return calls, try to place them yourself. If you must have your secretary make the call, then get on the line immediately. It's not polite to keep someone waiting when you've placed the call.

Good manners also dictate that you handle your mail promptly and courteously. Unless mail is obviously mass-produced, it should be deemed worthy of a reply. Most bosses don't like discovering that their employees are unresponsive to business calls and letters.

The arrival of fax machines and desktop computers in most offices has also given rise to a new etiquette regarding their use. Never assume that either a fax or e-mail is private. And with that in mind, never send any communication via either method that you wouldn't like to have your boss, or even your entire office, read. Most fax machines are located in public places, so anyone who passes by can read them, and some businesses routinely screen their employees' e-mail. (That's not necessarily polite, but it's easier to keep e-mail impersonal than to tell the boss she can't read it.)

≫ 3.6   Appointment Etiquette

The scheduling of appointments is very important in American culture. If you want to visit somebody or invite somebody to do something, the best way is to make appointment with him in advance, because most westerners often keep a strict personal schedule. They don't welcome unexpected visitors. Usually for a western businessman three schedules are kept: one for daily events, one for weekly planning, and one for long tern planning. You have to show respect for their cultural custom. Often appointments are made on the phone by talking with the person directly or with his secretary, who can help him to arrange the appointment. Remember to tell him or her directly why you want to meet him or her.

Don't be late for the appointment. You have to get to the meeting place on time. If something urgent happens which prevents you from keeping the appointment, you can change or cancel the appointment immediately. It is very impolite for you to fail to keep an appointment.

≫ 3.7   Some Tips for Office Etiquette

1) Top 10 Ways to Annoy Your Coworkers

Do you want to know how to make your coworkers hate you? Follow this advice. These are surefire ways to ensure your coworkers will look forward to the day you are gone. Avoid these behaviors if you want to help create harmony in your workplace.

a. Talk Loudly on Your Cell Phone ⋯ Especially in the Bathroom

Your coworkers don't want to listen to your cell phone conversations. They are not as entertaining to anyone as they are to you. More importantly, they don't want to hear you talk on your phone while you are in the bathroom. It makes them uncomfortable.

b. Take Credit for Your Coworkers' Contributions to a Project

When your boss congratulates you on a job well done, don't mention that you had a lot of help. Why does she need to know anyway? Team work, shmeam work. Better to look like you did it all on your own. And, when you need some help on the next project, where do you think your coworkers will be? Not on your team.

c. Come to Work Sick

If you have a cold or a stomach virus, spread it around. Your coworkers will thank you. On second thought, no, they won't. Well, hopefully they'll have the decency to call in sick and stop spreading the illness further.

d. Share Everything with Your Coworkers

Your coworkers are a curious bunch so it is in their best interests if you tell them everything about your personal life — even if, not make that especially if, it makes them uncomfortable. Your motto should be "too much information is never enough".

e. Talk to Your Coworkers About Religion and Politics

Ah, religion and politics … two topics about which everyone is in total agreement. Well, not exactly. Your coworkers may be very sensitive about these topics so if you want to offend them in a hurry, make sure they know why your beliefs are the only right ones.

f. Tell Your Coworkers Dirty Jokes

Everyone appreciates a good joke, right? That may be true, but while most people appreciate a good joke, many are put off by dirty jokes. It's not your problem so keep telling those jokes, but don't be surprised if you find yourself accused of sexual harassment one day.

g. Spam Your Coworkers

Forward tons of e-mail to all your coworkers. The content doesn't matter. Send it all — chain letters, jokes, and petitions. They'll be thinking of you as they keep hitting that delete button.

h. Chew Your Gum Loudly

Nothing sounds as yummy as the noise made by someone cracking their chewing gum and smacking their lips. It may drive your coworkers crazy, but isn't that what you're trying to do?

i. Don't Carry Your Own Weight

If you don't do your fair share of the work required by your department, your coworkers will have to pick up the slack. They'll be so exhausted from doing all the work, they won't be able to thank you.

j. Talk down to Your Coworkers

You may think talking down to your coworkers will build you up, but a condescending attitude will not make you appear stronger. It will, however, make your coworkers resent you.

2) How to Make Sure Your E-mail Gives a Good Impression

E-mail is increasingly becoming the primary way that many of us communicate with one another. Often, people never meet their colleagues or clients face-to-face or even talk to them on the telephone. The only impression others have of us may be the one they get when they read our e-mail messages. That is why it is so important to take great care in composing those messages. Before you hit the send button, ask yourself these questions.

a. What Does My E-Mail Address Say About Me?

If you are using your e-mail account to send professional e-mail, make sure your address conveys a professional tone. Don't use an address that is suggestive, childish, or cute. There is no place for that in work-related e-mail.

b. Are the Name and E-Mail Address in the "TO:" Field Correct?

Many e-mail clients fill in the "TO:" field for you when you type in the first few letters of an e-mail address or a recipient's name. Make sure the right name is there. You want to make sure your message reaches its intended destination, or that it doesn't reach an unintended one.

c. Have I Properly Addressed the Recipient?

First names are often okay in business, but not always. If this is your first time communicating with the recipient you should use his title, i. e., Mr., Ms., or Dr., and last name. Look at how the recipient signs his messages before you decide whether you should be on a first name basis with him.

d. Have I Used the Appropriate Tone?

As the saying goes, "It's not what you say but how you say it." It's a lot easier to convey the meaning of your words when you speak than when you write. Make sure your tone is polite and friendly, but gets across your intended meaning.

e. Is My E-Mail too Wordy (or Is It Not Wordy Enough)?

Get your point across quickly, but make sure not to leave out important details.

f. Have I Attached Unsolicited Attachments?

Many people won't, and shouldn't, open attachments they aren't expecting because computer viruses are often transmitted in them. Get permission from the recipient before attaching a file to your message.

≫ 3. 8   Sills and Strategies

1) Coworkers

(1) If you are aware of other people and do your part to make a good working environment, you should be able to get along with most of the people you work with.

(2) He's a hard worker, easy to get along with, honest, and he never steals the credit on projects.

(3) If you are negative and start name-calling in the office, it will make a bad working environment for everybody.

(4) One of the most important things is to be considerate of your coworkers' feelings and needs.

(5) The people in your department seem so capable and nice to be around.

(6) Some coworkers are harder to work with than others.

2) Bosses

(1) How are the things at the office lately?

(2) All of us at the office respect our boss a lot.

(3) You're lucky you can get along so well with your boss.

(4) He gave me so much work to do that afternoon that I didn't get around to meeting with the supervisor of our department.

(5) To deal with him every day, you should get a raise.

(6) It's your boss' responsibility to make sure employees are safe, and also doing their job.

3) Brainstorming

(1) I came up with a few different thoughts on the proposal.

(2) Maybe we do have some problems with time-management.

(3) Fifteen minutes would be good, but I wonder if it would make a big impact on the employees' output.

(4) We've got to come up with a way to solve this problem.

(5) We need to do some brainstorming to come up with a time-management solution for our office.

4) Commuting

(1) He commutes from the suburbs.

(2) It's not easy commuting every day, we should cut him some slack.

(3) He must get started on his commute about 6:30, no telling what time he actually gets up.

(4) While you're stressed out by your commute, I'm releasing all the stress of the day with mine.

(5) The commuting with public transportation is killing me.

5) The working lunch

(1) I've already had several days in a row working through lunch.

(2) Things are really busy for me today, the only time I can manage to squeeze out might be over lunch break.

(3) I hate to make you work through your lunch break.

(4) We can make it a working lunch this afternoon, and I'll order some Chinese food for delivery. It'll be my treat.

(5) Let's make it a date for Chop Suey and Martin account at about 12:30.

(6) Are you planning on treating the investors to a full-course meal?

Chapter 4

Business Etiquette
in Meeting

Business etiquette is essentially about building relationships with colleagues, clients or customers. In the business world, it is these people that can influence your success or failure. Etiquette, and in particular business etiquette, is simply a means of maximizing your business potential by presenting yourself favorably.

≫ 4. 1　The Definition of Business Meeting Etiquette

Business meeting etiquette refers to the proper way that people handle themselves in a business and social environment, which can range from meetings with the boss to meetings with clients and customers and knowing the right things to do and to say. It includes the good manners for both formal meeting and informal meeting.

If a company is planning a business meeting, they need to review etiquette for conducting one. They should follow business meeting protocol and ensure their guests and important speakers feel appreciated and important to the success of the business, which will help the meeting run smoothly.

According to business meeting etiquette, meeting leaders should sit at the head table of a business meeting, which shows to the meeting attendees who will lead the meeting and to whom they should listen and direct questions about the meeting agenda.

If there is a guest speaker for the meeting or another important speaker, give the head seat to this person. If you are the meeting leader, sit beside the guest speaker. As the speaker, you may also take the head position and place the guest speaker beside you.

If the meeting will be held in a global setting, check with a person who works in the company in the country in which you are visiting to find out what kinds of specific business etiquette rules it inhabitants observe.

Using round table to negotiate a deal can eliminate the "head position", thus make the employees feel equal. Being a meeting leader at the round table, you should assert yourself and bring an agenda, which will signal to employees that you are chairing the meeting.

Wearing proper business attire is also very important at the business meeting. As the person sitting in the head position at the table, dress appropriately. Dressing in a suit indicates that you care about your job and are professional, responsible and a strong leader.

≫ 4. 2　Some Basic Rules on Business Meeting Etiquette

Business meetings are one arena in which poor etiquette can have negative effects. By improving your business meeting etiquette, you automatically improve your chances of success. Comfort, trust, attentiveness and clear communication are examples of the positive results of demonstrating good etiquette.

The following are some basic rules on business meeting etiquette for both formal and informal business meetings and they are meant as guides to etiquette that are very much applicable to any nations in the world.

1) Informal Meetings

Informal meetings are generally more relaxed affairs and may not necessarily take place in the office or meeting room. Even so a sense of professionalism and good business etiquette are still required. There are 7 points to consider with informal meetings:

● Business etiquette demands that the person calling the meeting (henceforth "the chair") should be the most senior or the one with the most direct or urgent interest in the topic at hand.

● The chair should decide the time, place and agenda. These details should be confirmed with everyone to make sure all are in agreement and no inconvenience is caused.

● The chair must make the purpose of the meeting clear to the attendees, how long it will last and what is expected of them, i. e. , particular information or preparation of documents. Failing to relay the proper information is bad business etiquette as it could cause embarrassment.

● Punctuality is a must. Keeping people waiting is considered the height of poor etiquette as it abuses their time.

● The chair should strive to ensure the meeting stays within a set framework or agenda so that it is kept as short and effective as possible. He/she must keep circular disagreements and the like to a minimum.

● The chair should appoint someone to record the proceedings; documenting major decisions or action points. This can later be distributed to the attendees for reference.

● If the results of the meeting have an effect on others who were not present it is considered proper business etiquette to inform them.

2) Formal Meetings

The business etiquette of formal meetings such as departmental meetings, management meetings, board meetings, negotiations and the like can be puzzling. Such meetings usually have a set format. For example, the chair may always be the same person, minutes, agendas or reports may be pre-distributed or voting may take place. Here are 10 business etiquette guidelines that are applicable to any formal meeting:

● Prepare well for the meeting as your contribution may be integral to the proceedings. If you are using statistics, reports or any other information make sure it has been handed out at least three days prior to the meeting.

● Dress well and arrive in good time. Your professionalism is linked to both.

● Always remember to switch of a mobile phone.

● If there is an established seating pattern, accept it. If you are unsure, ask.

● Acknowledge any introductions or opening remarks with a brief recognition of the chair and other participants.

● When discussions are under way it is good business etiquette to allow more senior figures to contribute first.

● Never interrupt anyone — even if you disagree strongly. Note what has been said and return to it later with the chair's permission.

● When speaking, be brief and ensure what you say is relevant.

● Always address the chair unless it is clear that others are not doing so.

● It is a serious breach of business etiquette to divulge information to others about a meeting. What has been discussed should be considered as confidential.

The underlying principles of the all the above business meeting etiquette pointers are good manners, courtesy and consideration. If these principles are adhered to, the chances of offense and misunderstandings are greatly reduced.

≫ 4.3   Some Guidelines on Business Meeting Etiquette

Business meeting etiquette is basically good common sense, but one that takes a little practice. Certainly, we can all identify what *not* to do when planning and/or attending a meeting, but often what we really need is a set of guidelines as to how to do this successfully. Here are some tips to help.

1) Attending a Meeting

a. Be on Time

Always arrive a few minutes before the meeting is set to begin. This indicates respect for the person planning the meeting and shows that you are organized.

b. Be Prepared

Before the meeting, be sure to read any related material or review policies and procedures that will be addressed. You will be much better able to provide valuable input.

c. Bring a Notebook and Pen

Even if you don't take a single note, this will show that you are interested in the agenda and serious about your role at the meeting.

d. Participate

When the chairperson asks for feedback and you feel that you have something to contribute, be sure to do so. Ask questions as well.

e. Be Polite and Attentive

Never engage in cross-talk in a meeting and be courteous to the person who has the floor. Listen to what is being said and resist the urge to argue with anyone.

f. Conduct Yourself Professionally

Meetings are a great place to let people know that you are serious and have something to offer. Use this opportunity to demonstrate your knowledge and understanding.

g. Thank the Chairperson

It's such a little thing, but thanking the person who organized the meeting is not only good etiquette, it is also a sign of respect.

2) Running a Meeting

a. Plan Ahead

If you are responsible for calling a meeting, plan ahead before sending out the meeting notification. Make sure that all interested parties are invited.

b. Set a Clear Agenda

In your meeting invitation, clearly state the agenda of the meeting. List the action items and request that attendees come prepared to address these issues. Attach related documentation for review and request input.

c. Set a Time Limit

In today's business environment, everyone is busy. By setting a clear time limit, you are showing that you respect your coworkers' need for time management as well as your own.

d. Dress Professionally

You want to be taken seriously, and appearance is important. Even if it is "casual Friday," wear appropriate business apparel.

e. Encourage Punctuality

Never be late to your own meeting! Set an example and plan to be in the room a few minutes before the start time.

f. Manage the Meeting

Stick to the agenda and keep an eye on the time. Politely discourage cross-talk and make sure that every person has an opportunity to speak. Move the agenda along, but not so fast as to miss key points. If the meeting goes off-topic, remind the group of the agenda at hand and suggest that unrelated matters be addressed at another time.

g. Avoid Engaging in Petty Bickering or Arguments

Remain calm and diplomatic, no matter how heated the discussion may become.

h. Summarize

At the end of the meeting, sum up the action items and if necessary, request another meeting.

i. Follow-up

Once the meeting is over, follow up with all attendees. Send a list of action items, resolutions and issues that remain open. Thank people for taking the time to attend, and request feedback.

≫ 4.4　Attending on International Conference

A business meeting is formal, especially when it is a meeting between people from separate companies. Formal introductions and exchange of business cards are usually done at the start of the meeting. The organizer keeps the pace of the meeting and makes the meeting as efficient as possible.

Attending on international conference is a big event. There are a number of things to take care when attending. We will try to highlight some of the items for attending conferences.

When attending on international conference, you are attending as a scholar or a businessman. Confidence is everything. To be confident, you should prepare well.

Presentation is a skill that did not receive much attention in the Chinese universities. In the United States, almost every department of Humanities in the universities offers Public Speaking class. Most people need to be trained for this skill.

When you first come to the stage for presentation, take a deep breath, and start talking when you are ready. Do not be scared by the eyes of the audience. Make eye contacts with them. Use your gesture and high and low tones of voice. Make sure the microphone works before you start talking. If you can hear your voice quite loud, you feel you have power and control of the presentation, which makes you confident. Don't be afraid that you repeated something. To get your ideas across, there are at least three things that you repeat three times in a presentation.

≫ **4. 5 Successful Meetings**

While effective meetings are essential to any organization and to getting work done, most meetings leave us still looking for a decision, tired and in need of a chiropractor. A good meeting, like a football team's huddle, should bring people together, facilitate decision making, assist people in taking responsibility, energize the participants, and contribute to building team effort within the organization.

Successful meetings are ones where attention is paid to three areas: content, design and process.

Selection of content is crucial. All too often meetings are called to discuss issues which would be better resolved with a couple of phone calls while at the same time core issues remain unmentioned. The key is to focus meetings around key issues, the ones that motivate employees and to let the meeting participants identify the priority of items to be addressed.

Secondly, the design of the meeting can hinder or support the decision making, problem solving or the informational task at hand. In designing attention needs to be given to idea generation methods, decision processes, agenda, time frames, problem-solving steps, etc.

Third, and most often ignored, is making sure the individual and group needs of the participants are met. Are people participating, included, feeling that there is room for their ideas? Are dysfunctional behaviors openly dealt with, is there positive energy in the group, are people committed to the task at hand and enthused about the way the group is working to complete the task?

Common Mistakes:
- Trying to facilitate a meeting and be a participant at the same time.
- Discussion of multiple ideas at once.
- Lack of agreement on how decisions will be made.

Putting a Price on Meeting Productivity:
- The Wharton Centre for Applied Research published the following findings in the *Wall Street Journal*.
- The average chief executive officer spends about 17 hours each week in meetings.
- Senior executives spend an average of 23 hours a week in meetings.
- Middle managers spend 11 hours in meetings per week.
- Senior and middle managers said only 56% of meetings were productive.

They added that a phone call or a memo could have replaced over 25% of the meetings they attend.

Using this data we know that if managers use meetings appropriately they can reduce the time spent in meetings by 25%. Effective management of remaining meetings can reduce time spent in meetings by an additional 20% . This indicates that using meetings effectively results in a reduction of time spent in meetings from an average of 17 hours per week to 10 hours per week.

If managers plan and conduct meetings effectively they can end up with 7 additional hours per week to get other work done! And the annual benefit of improving meeting productivity is a whopping $ 9 ,000 to $ 16 ,000 per manager.

≫ 4. 6   Some Tips for Business Meeting Etiquette

Business meetings are loved as a way out of mundane work by some. They are dreaded interruptions by others. Regardless of the quality of the topic or the entertainment value in the presentation — for better or worse — you can likely learn something to enhance your career.

Here are five tips to make sure you are a superstar in the meeting:

1) Punctuality Is Priority

Be on time. Be early. Arriving late is not only rude to your boss, your meeting leader, yourself, but it is also rude to the other participants. Why? Because it often requires attention being moved from the topic of discussion to the rude late-comer shuffling in, people often do not get ahead by having "that" kind of attention!

2) Avoid Electronic Distraction

Unless you are invited to record or take photos and videos of the discussion — keep your cell phones and other distractions turned off. If you need your PDA function for note taking — silence it. No one wants to hear "Mama Said Knock You Out" when your mom calls to complain about how you don't call enough. It's also not cute to hear the "beep, boop, bong, bleep" as you type. Cut it out. Put it on silent.

3) Prepare to Be Productive

If you were given a meeting agenda before hand, study it and know your opinion on key points before the meeting begins. Know the news of the day and how it relates to your company, and the meeting topic. If called on, don't be afraid to take a beat to collect your thoughts before speaking your mind. The more prepared you are beforehand, the more you appear unflappable and an asset to the group.

4) No Signs of Gum

I don't care if you're on the latest "all gum" diet or not — the presenter should not be aware of your gum in a professional meeting. If they can notice it — it's rude. No smacking, or bubbles, or popping — which is easiest to avoid these subconscious habits by not chewing gum in meetings at all. And whatever you do, do not be the "crinkler." Do not be the attendee that disturbs the neighboring participants by opening candy and gum while the speaker is conducting the meeting.

  * If you happen to be diabetic — attend to your blood sugar level before the meeting & have something discrete handy in case of an emergency.

5) Pay Attention like Your Career Depends on It

Seriously, it might! Take notes and pay enough attention that you could sum up the key points for colleagues that were unable to attend. And really drink in the subjects that can be applied to your job functions.

Your behavior in meetings and conferences could have a serious effect on your career. In both directions! Be on your best behavior, your success may depend on it!

≫ 4. 7   Skills andStrategies

1) A preface to asking a question

(1) Excuse me…
(2) Pardon me…
(3) Excuse me for asking…
(4) If you don't mind my asking…
(5) It's none of my business, but…

2) A preface to making a statement

(1) IfI may say so….
(2) If it's okay with you…
(3) Please be advised that…
(4) It is a pleasure to inform you that…
(5) As you may already know…

3) Announcing a meeting open

(1) Ladies and gentlemen,
  My name is Jim Miller, from the head office , and I'm going to chair this morning's session.
  It's my pleasure to welcome you, my colleagues from all over the world, to our conference.
  Now I declare the meeting open.
(2) According to the order of the program today, I will be responsible for this session. I would

like to ask your kind cooperation.

(3) Ladies and gentlemen:

We shall start our main business. Today we should like, first of all, to discuss the problem of marketing. All are urged to exchange their ideas frankly regarding the problems we now face.

3) Calling on the participants to speak

(1) All are encouraged to frankly exchange ideas.

(2) We sincerely hope that all present here will feel free to express your ideas and exchange opinions, so as to make this conference a real success.

(3) The topic of our conference is to how to promote our cooperation. Let's discuss all our problems frankly and clearly, and in this way, work towards a solution.

(4) What did everyone think of the presentation just now? We also would like to hear from nonmember participants present here.

4) Reminding the speaker

(1) I'm afraid what you said is beside the point. It seems to me there is no connection between your words and topic presently being discussed.

(2) I'm afraid your speech is very general. Could you please make your point more concretely?

(3) Somewhat it seems that what has just been said falls a bit beyond the range of our present topic. Let's go back to the main theme.

5) Adjourning or closing a meeting

(1) Ladies and gentlemen, the meeting is now adjourning. Thank you all for your cooperation.

(2) I thought I'd now briefly summarize what have been said so far... Our time is up. So let us end our discussion at this point for the time being.

(3) I think that covers everything on today's agenda. Our next meeting will be on Monday morning, at the same time and place. Let's call it a day.

Chapter 5 · Business Etiquette in Communication

In general, organizations are seeking to capture new market space for their business, services and brands; there has never been a more pertinent time to ensure the highest levels of business success from every activity undertaken. The current economic climate around the world is requiring a higher level of communication, cross-cultural understanding and people management than ever before. Each marketplace has its own parameters for how business people in it like to be communicated with. It is a vital prerequisite for business people to now "do business" with a greater knowledge, understanding and respect for different cultures.

>>> 5.1 The Definition of Communication Etiquette

Business communication etiquette refers to a kind of standard behavior observed by the businessmen in their communication; it also is a kind of civilization accumulation of people which has to do with good manners that have a very practical value in the business word. It involves certain universally applicable and acceptable rules which are indispensable in the business circle.

As a businessman, you must be aware that any communication needs etiquette which can reflects your personal self-cultivation. Most successful business activities are based upon successful communication. If you want to achieve success in business deal, you must have a good command of the etiquette.

In general, communication etiquette consists of two kinds: language etiquette and non-language etiquette. As we know language is a system of symbols people use to communicate and communication is a bilateral process that takes place when information is exchanged, understanding is promoted, and questions are answered. The process requires motive participation between a speaker and listener. The quality of one's communication depends on the level of his/her commitment to the process. Thus, language in business communication should be appropriate and courteous. While non-language etiquette refers to nonverbal communicating etiquette which concerns courteous of sight, facial expression, gestures, body space and silence. Non-language courtesy varies from one culture to another, and it is regarded as a sort of real art. For example, a gesture of happiness in one culture may be a kind of rude manner in another culture, no means agreement in the USA and Canada but it means disagreement in Nepal and Bulgaria.

A successful communication can both bring you great interpersonal relationship and facilitate carrying out your business activities. Observing etiquette in business communication requires both parties to pay attention to the language they use and the speed they speak. In addition, a businessman should choose the right topic and right place. During the communication, the facial expressions of both parties should be noticed and the topics and atmosphere can be changed in time.

All in all, communication etiquette is the proper behavior that should be followed in the business world; it is the way that you handle yourself in a business and social environment.

≫ 5.2　Effective Communication—Good Listening

Good listening is crucial to effective communication and career success. Most of us don't know how to listen intelligently, systematically and purposefully.

Think about your most recent conversations at work or at home. If you remember what you said better than what you heard, you've probably developed some bad listening habits. Instead of really listening, you let your mind wander while others were talking. You were thinking about what you were going to say before the others had finished.

Faulty listening habits can cause misunderstandings several times a day in a busy office. Indeed, many serious mistakes and organizational mix-ups stem from someone not hearing instructions. Poor listening can cause snafus such as missing important appointments, misunderstanding directions, misinterpreting valuable suggestions or addressing the wrong problems.

There is little doubt that poor listening habits have killed many managerial careers. The higher the manager is on the corporate ladder, the more time he or she spends listening to others. Interestingly, most executive-appraisal studies find that managers who are rated most efficient by subordinates are good listeners.

Becoming aware of deficient listening skills, coupled with a conscious effort at overcoming them, will help you master the art of listening. The following guidelines are useful in improving listening efficiency:

1) Increase Your Listening Skills

Interrupting and finishing a speaker's sentences often damage communication. Deliberately try to inhibit your temptation to interrupt. Make sure the speaker has finished conveying the message before you speak.

By your actions, show the speaker you are genuinely interested and want to listen. If you aren't sure of the whole message, ask the speaker to repeat or clarify it. Constantly evaluate your own understanding of the message.

The most effective way to break the interrupting habit is to apologize every time you interrupt. After a few apologies, you'll think twice before jumping in while a person is speaking.

2) Take Time to Listen

The speaker is apt to feel rushed if you indicate your listening time is limited. Many people think aloud and grope toward their meaning. Frequently, initial statements only vaguely approximate what a person means. For the speaker to open up and crystallize the meaning, you must convey that you have time to talk freely.

Don't rationalize that you're too busy to listen. Instead, set aside whatever you're doing. This will reassure the speaker that he doesn't have to talk faster or abbreviate the message. It will also help you to concentrate on what's being said.

3) Give Your Full Attention

You will act like a good listener if you are alert, look the speaker in the eye and lean forward. Radiate interest by nodding your head or raising your eyebrows, and offer encouragement with comments and questions such as, "Is that what you had in mind?" and "Check my understanding, but I think you're telling me …" followed by a paraphrase of the speaker's remarks.

4) Adapt Your Thought Speed

You can think three to four times faster than a person can talk, which is a major reason for poor concentration. Impatient with the speaker's slow progress, your mind wanders off until you hear something that interests you. Then you realize you've missed something, and you don't really understand what the person is asking. When the temptation to take brief mental excursions becomes irresistible — this frequently happens while listening to long-winded speakers — your listening efficiency drops to near zero.

To use your thinking speed to advantage, keep analyzing what the speaker's saying as he talks. Mentally sum up what's been said. Weigh the evidence by considering whether the facts are accurate and the viewpoints are objective, or whether the speaker is only trying to prove a point.

5) Don't Overreact to the Delivery

If you become too involved in a person's speech style, you will lose track of the message. Force yourself to concentrate on the message instead of the speaker's accent or style of speaking, speech impediment or disorganized thought pattern. Ask yourself: "What is he or she saying that I need to know?"

6) Listen Between the Lines

Concentrate not only on what's being said but also on the attitudes, needs and motives behind the words. Remember that the speaker's words may not always contain the entire message. The changing tones and volume of the speaker's voice may have meaning. So may facial expressions, gestures and body movements. Being alert to nonverbal cues increases your total comprehension of the message.

For example, sometimes the message and auditory and behavioral cues differ considerably. Although the speaker says he is excited about an idea or project, his lack of spontaneous movement, wandering or downcast eyes, unanimated tone of voice, masked face or hunched posture may indicate he feels differently.

Relying on words alone is like trying to work a jigsaw puzzle with many pieces missing. You get the general idea but there are gaps you can't fill.

7) Don't Become Distracted

Poor listeners are distracted by sounds, objects and people, such as a police siren, a telephone ringing or a person passing in the hallway. Good listeners position themselves to avoid distractions or concentrate harder on what the speaker is saying.

≫ 5. 3   Excellent Business Communication

The idea that people need to have feedback, appreciation and information is a good basis for understanding how and why excellent business communication is important and compelling for success.

In your very best relationship — whether your spouse, best friend, sister, coworker — you can easily communicate with them in a high value way. You telephone, e-mail, write notes, make plans and generally stay in contact with them because you want a connection and a relationship with them.

In building very good relationships in business, it is absolutely the same. What is different in a business relationship is that you are communicating with colleagues and you don't always know them as well as a dear friend. However, they need the same attention that a good relationship needs. These needs are:

- returning a phone call.
- following up on a request.
- listening intently.
- appreciative communication.
- clearing communication with details and directions.

- doing what you say you will do.
- remembering what is important to them.
- valuing what is most important to them.

Our communication styles and methods are being stretched by e-mail, technology, lack of time and resources that limit our ability to do so much in our day. But there are rules of common courtesy that have NOT changed since the inception of humans dealing with each other in a high value way. If you want to be a remembered, trusted and respected leader, you will practice these courtesies with every business contact.

If you take the time to examine what is important to you, you will find that they are also the courtesies that you expect in all business communication, actually how you would like to be treated and communicated with.

E-mail — Not only should you be returning e-mails in a timely way, but you need to set the context each and every time of why the e-mail is important and what information it is that you want to deliver. Spam filters help, but in order to more easily control your e-mail load, you need to be in more control of what you generate yourself. In business, be brief, be informational and be gone.

Cell phones — The ring tones that are available now are fun outside of the office, networking situations, client lunches, etc. Put your cell phone on manner mode or shut it off. Take and make calls when you are with people sparingly. Most people are not interested in listening to your phone conversation no matter how stimulating you think they might be. If you need to take or make a call, excuse yourself and then make it brief.

Returning phone calls — Whether you think you have time to return the call or not, find out what people need, make sure you are clear on whether you can help them or not and then get back to your own work. People who return phone calls are trusted and respected. You do not need to make the calls long. In fact, returning all calls twice a day instead of doing it piece meal all day long is a good way to manage your time more appropriately.

Here are some additional basics that will help you grow your own identity and brand which will identify you as a trusted and respected up and coming leader:

Practice your handshake — Ask a friend to shake hands with you and then give you feedback. Firm is good.

Eye contact — Learn to look at a person when they are speaking.

Body language — 55% of our nonverbal communication is our body. Watch what your body is saying about you.

Business cards — Get one and have them with you ALL of the time. You should include an address, e-mail, telephone number, full name, what you do and your title. If your company does not provide a business card, get one for you anyway. The fast print companies all have programs you can easily and quickly make one for you.

Holding doors — Opening a door for someone is not just a guy thing anymore. Ladies, if you get to the door first, open it.

≫ 5. 4   Proper Business Communication Manners

Whether you are aware of it or not, first impression does make a major difference in achieving business objectives. Having good manners will help you regardless of the business you are in. Any time you make contact with a client or perspective client, you are making a mini-presentation of yourself, ultimately representing your company, service and/or products.

But how can you mind your manners, if you do not know the rules. It is never too late to take the initiative to begin your own professional development. Here are some pointers to keep your manners sharp.

1) Address Individuals by Their Honorific or Title

There is so much informality in the workplace today that in many offices business is lost, and goodwill destroyed, because of total disregard for properly addressing clients. The proper way to address a client is to greet them using their honorific or title followed by their last name. It is up to the client to ask you to call them by their first name.

In business, the proper way to refer to a woman is "Ms. ," regardless of their marital status. This is more than a passing fad; it was established in the seventeenth century as an abbreviation for "Mistress. "

2) Enunciate Your Greeting

When we introduce ourselves or other people, we need to slow down and pronounce our names slowly, clearly and distinctly. At first it may feel as if you are exaggerating your name, but you are really helping the other person and improving overall communication.

3) Refer to Individuals Frequently by Their Names

Take the time and make the effort to pay attention to the name of the person you are being introduced to. A person's name means everything to them. To build rapport with a client, mention their name at least three times during the conversation. It will help you remember their name and make a connection — they will remember you. A person's name is the sweetest music to their ears.

4) Make Contact

There are few physical contacts that are appropriate in business; the most important and acceptable is your handshake. Your handshake is a non-verbal clue that indicates to the other person whether or not you are a take charge person. For example, a firm and strong handshake suggests that you are decisive, in control. Now think of the impression you had after shaking hands with someone that presented a weak, slippery or lifeless handshake. What did that make you think of them?

5) Shake Hands

The rules for shaking hands are: extend your hand with the thumb up, clasp the other person's entire palm, give two or three pumps from the elbow, avoiding both the painful "bone crusher" and the off-putting "wet fish" shake, and look at the person directly in the eyes with a smile.

6) Smile

This seems very simple, but it's amazing how people's moods and words are misjudged because their expressions are often overly-serious. A smile shows that you like yourself; you like your current place in the world and you're happy with the people you're interacting with. No one will say you're crabby if you're smiling. A smile says, I'm approachable and confident.

7) Make Eye Contact

Every time a person begins talking to you, look them in the eye and smile first, then get on with the conversation. Also, when you enter a room for a meeting, smile and look around at everyone. If you want to start talking to one person — or even a group — come up to them and smile. Again, this is another way to say, I'm approachable.

8) Introduce People with Confidence

Most people hate making introductions, because they do not know how to properly make them. Introducing people with confidence is a great way to impress your customers. In business, introductions are determined by precedence. The person who holds the position of highest authority in an organization takes precedence over others who work there. For example, you introduce your company's president to a colleague.

The basic rule is: the name of the person of **greater authority** is always spoken first. The name of the person of **lesser authority** is always spoken last. For example, "*Mr. /Ms. Greater Authority, I would like to introduce Mr. /Ms. Lesser Authority*". A second example would be: the name of the **Senior Executive** is always spoken first. The name of the **Junior Executive** is always spoken last. "*Mr. Senior Executive, I would like to introduce Mr. Junior Executive, from the accounting department. Mr. Senior Executive is our Director of Public Relations*".

Learning the rules of business etiquette is not hard to do, it is not costly, and it is the best professional development tool any business person can use to increase their chances of success. People truly desire to do business with those that make them comfortable and know how to best handle themselves in a variety of situations. Practicing good business etiquette is well worth the investment and pays back in spades.

≫ 5.5   Communicating Etiquette

The way you communicate in writing or over the phone is sometimes more important than communication in person. This is because people may not be able to see your body language or hear your tone of voice. So word choice is imperative. Avoid ambiguity and jokes that could be misinterpreted.

1) Letter Format

Letters are still the most formal mode of communication, though they are seldom used now with electronic types of communication. Even with e-mail, it is still important to know the format of a formal business letter:

- Use 8 1/2 by 11 inch paper.
- Write in single space
  If the letter is not printed on letterhead, type your address, not including your name, at the top of the letter.
- Skip one line. Then write out the date.
- Skip one line. Then type the recipients name, title, and address.
- Skip one line. Write the salutation, including the recipient's title, last name, and a colon. For example, write, "Dear Mr. Peterson".
- Skip one line. Write the short body of the letter.
  In the **first part** state the purpose of the letter and identify your connection to the recipient. In the **second part**, describe what you want. In the **third part**, make the specific request. Skip **two** lines. Close your letter with "Yours truly" or "Sincerely". Then skip three lines to leave room for your signature, and type your name.

2) E-mails

Many people think that e-mails can be more casual and less grammatically correct than writing letters or speaking in person. That may be true in the case of friends or family; however, in business e-mail you should not address the recipient in a more casual tone than you would in person. And though e-mail is a quick and convenient mode of communication, you should still use correct English. Take time to check for spelling, grammar, and proper usage.

3) Faxes

Faxes are great for sending quick copies, but unsolicited faxes can be very annoying. When faxing, always send a cover sheet indicating the number of pages being faxed. Never send more than five pages without notifying the recipient before hand.

4) Phones

Lately more and more business transactions are done over the phone, and phone interviews are a pretty common procedure. So know the proper protocol.

5) Making Calls

- Be mentally prepared to make a call before you dial. Know with whom you want to speak and what you want to say or ask.
- Always introduce yourself right away.
- When leaving messages, speak slowly, and leave your number twice: once at the beginning of the message and once at the end.

6) Receiving Calls

- If you are actively job seeking, leave an application log next to your phone. Having quick information about the status of an application will save you from having to ask recruiters to tell you who they are and will keep you from seeming unorganized or desperate.
- When receiving calls for others find out who's calling before you say whether or not the person is in. When asking who is calling make sure to ask permission to ask; that is, phrase your question something like this: "May I ask who's calling?" This will avoid alienating the caller.

7) Cell Phones

- Turn your cell phone off during meetings; answering your cell phone in a meeting gives the impression that those around you are less important than any other person who might call.
- Try not to answer the phone when you are in restaurants; if you are expecting an important call, let those you are dining with know, and when you receive the call, excuse yourself, leave the table, and make the call brief.
- Be aware of how loud you talk on a cell phone in public places and create space by moving at least two arm lengths away from those around you (or out of the room if possible).

≫ 5.6　Some Rules for Proper Office Communication

Developing and communicating a set of shared expectations can create a more positive office atmosphere. Such "rules" reintroduce a sense of predictability, lower stress and allow people to focus more on the tasks at hand. Here are rules for proper office etiquette including e-mail and cell phone use, and other interactions with coworkers:

1) Appearances Count

With people working various schedules, it becomes difficult to simply track down the people you need to see at any given time. For example, if one person drives to the office to collaborate with others who are working at home that day, the effort is wasted. To save coordination time, it is helpful to set core hours or core days when each member of a work group will be on-site, or otherwise available. Regardless of how your organization decides to handle flexible work arrangements, there are several group behaviors that can smooth the way:

● Always use sign-out boards (electronic if possible). This allows coworkers to quickly and easily locate each other.

● Have a predetermined method of notifying other group members if a person decides to work at home; how to notify, who to notify, when to notify, contact information if you find out that coworkers are inheriting your calls and crises when you work away from the main office, take on extra tasks that help them, or cut back voluntarily on time away until a fair way to manage this overflow can be worked out.

● Coordinate set work times for your administrative support person to be available to the work group. For example, if the group routinely needs secretarial help preparing for early-morning meetings, flexibility for the secretary to show up later will cause frequent disappointments. Take the time to work this out before trouble starts.

● Dressing for success no longer means formality. But if you are meeting with customers or others who expect more formality, dress appropriately. If your organization has a dress code, find out what it is.

● If you have the option to set your own hours, don't abuse the system or become unavailable. If this way of working does not get results or causes workgroup problems, everybody suffers and formality has a way of returning.

2) Let's Meet

Meetings are frequently named as the biggest office time wasters. They don't need to be. With people working different hours, meetings are more important than ever as a way to set project directions and get to know coworkers. Consistent meeting behavior helps make this time count.

● Be on time. Busy people don't want to wait and will bail out if others don't show up.

● If meetings routinely don't start when scheduled, people will stop taking meeting notices seriously and nobody will show up.

● Plan ahead when it's your meeting. Check the space before the meeting starts to be sure needed equipment is there and working. Are markers, flip charts or other needed supplies in the space? Do you have enough copies of handouts?

● Start and end meetings as scheduled. People have other places to be and other things to do.

● If you don't need a full hour, just schedule 30 minutes and end even sooner if you can.

● Get to the point. First announce the purpose and the desired outcome of the meeting. When you've reached your desired outcome, end the meeting.

● Turn off your phone during meetings. Your conversation about the taking the dog to the vet is not pertinent to the other people at the table. If something truly urgent does, come up, leave the meeting and attend to it privately.

● If the meeting space is tucked into an area of cubicles, be aware that people are trying to concentrate. If the meeting cannot be conducted at conversational volume levels, move the meeting to a space where the noise will not disrupt others.

If you rearrange a meeting space, put it back into usable order before leaving. Erase marker boards, take down charts and clear up all papers, etc. If you borrow items from other meeting spaces, return them promptly.

3) Let's Eat

In many offices, people often work through lunch and dinner; eating snacks, even elaborate desktop dinners at their workstation. Food is often catered in, and snack machines are everywhere. The result is an all-day cacophony of soda HISSES, microwave BEEPS, CRUNCHING, MUNCHING and the BANG-SCRAPE-BANG of silverware on dishes. Add a variety of strong food aromas, and you have a recipe for workgroup distraction.

● Don't use china and silverware within 50 feet of anyone who's trying to concentrate.

● If you want formal dining, go out.

● Use office areas outside of workstations for lunch. It's better ergonomically to take a break, and routinely eating quickly is not healthy. If there is no café, break space or cafeteria, find a spot outside or by a window. Or take the opportunity to interact with others over lunch in a casual space.

● If you have to eat at your desk, choose "quiet" foods. Cut back on the crunchy stuff. Stirring ice tea with a vengeance is also hard on group peace. Also think twice about foods that have strong odors — remember that other people will have to live with those odors all afternoon.

● Get a grip. Coworkers may be trying to cut back on fat, salt and calories. If you are choosing food for a meeting, offer healthy options and/or agree as a group on whether the meeting needs to include food.

● Be respectful to the next group to use a teaming space. Always clean up unless you know there is a cleaning crew on the way.

4) Cube Life

58% of American offices use some type of open plan layout. Commonly called cubicles, these workstations offer some privacy, but typically do not have doors or ceilings. Although open plan layouts increase collaboration, they also require basic consideration of others.

- Respect others' privacy. Don't borrow items from other peoples' workstations or hover over their shoulder while they finish a phone call. Never open drawers or cabinets in other peoples' stations without permission.
- Never use a computer without permission. "PC" stands for "Personal Computer," surprise visitors are rarely welcome.
- If you do have permission to use someone's PC, remember that settings should not be changed without the owner's knowledge. E-mail and files should be considered confidential and off limits.
- Your organization may have some rules about decorating. Check with your facilities person or coworkers to determine what the corporate culture accommodates. Even if there is no written policy, pictures or other items that could offend coworkers are never a good idea.
- Music should be played on headphones, not speakers — tastes in music vary too much for anyone to choose for a whole group.
- If you share a cubicle, remember to clean up after yourself each time you leave and store shared materials where the coworker will be able to find them.
- When using a shared printer, reload paper when it's your turn and save huge print jobs for times when your work group will not be in a hurry for printed documents.
- Just because you have some visual privacy, don't assume your annoying habits are a secret. Chewing ice and clipping nails are not ways to make friends in open plans.
- Respect your coworkers' concentration. If you see someone deeply involved in typing, reading or thinking, come back later or send an e-mail if possible.
- Using speakerphones keeps your hands free, but ties up both ears of every coworker in your immediate area. Not a good tradeoff — pick up the receiver, or get a headset.
- Group cultures vary. In some organizations it's OK to carry on a discussion with someone ten-feet away. In others, that would cause distraction. Pay attention to the conduct in your office and if there's a problem, talk it over with your work group.

5) Virtual and Part-time Life

Some workers are on the road four days a week or more. They do not need to maintain personal space at the office, but do need to stop in occasionally for meetings or administrative tasks. Others' work may work part time schedules. Etiquette tips for virtual workers:

- If there is a concierge or reservation system, make your plans known before your arrival.
- Vacate spaces when you said you would, unless nobody is waiting for the space.
- Clean up your belongings when you leave and return borrowed items.
- Leave contact information for people to reach you while you are out.
- Etiquette tips for part-time or variable-schedule workers.
- Remember to view your involvement from the group's perspective. Don't just rush in and announce what you need from them while explaining that you don't have time to help them.

Show some give and take.

● Let coworkers know your work schedule. Block out all non-work times on electronic calendar systems and/or post a work schedule in your workstation.

● Clean up after yourself before leaving and delegate things that could need attention while you are out. Leave tracks. For example, if you have the key to a supply cabinet and will be out for three days, who takes the key during that time?

● The more our work styles change, the more new issues will come up. Flexible work styles often communicate that the individual is the center of a universe and that group norms are no longer important. With some patience and consideration of others however, the workplace can remain a comfortable and productive place for everyone.

≫ 5. 7   Some Tips for Business Communication

When we communicate with foreign business counterparts, we have to remember the following pointers:

1) Making Contact

● Try not to make assumptions about a person's degree of deaf blindness.
● Take your time and explain things clearly at a pace the person can follow.
● Avoid shouting.
● Try not to place your hands over your mouth.
● If the person cannot hear speech you can approach them by gently touching the back of the person's hand.
● Even if using an interpreter, direct your communication at the individual.
● Let the person know when you enter and leave a room.

2) Environment

● Consider the physical layout of an environment including the positioning of furniture and any clutter around the floor.
● Allow the person to become familiar with the environment.
● Inform and show the person if there are any changes to the environment.

3) Lighting and Contrast

● Position yourself in the light.
● Avoid having your back to a window.
● Ask the person if the lighting is suitable.
● Create contrast between yourself and the background.

4) Glare

- Avoid glare and lights that shine directly into a person's eyes.
- If guiding a person from inside to outside ask if they are ready to move on as people need time to adjust to changes in light.

5) Background Noise

- Reduce any unnecessary background noise.

6) Locating Personal Belongings

- Let the person know where their belongings can be found.

7) Anticipating What Is Happening Next

- Let the person know what is about to happen. Do not assume that they know.

8) Tactile Cues

- Consider the range of tactile cues in the environment (e. g. , present a cup to ask a person if they would like a drink).

9) Asking Questions

- Asking questions encourages two way communications.
- Ask whether they have any questions.

10) Choice

- Where possible present the person with choices and allow them the opportunity to make their own decisions.

11) Access to Information

- Ensure that individuals have easy access to information.

12) Relaying Non-verbal Messages

- Describe non-verbal cues in the environment such as other people's facial expressions and the content of written material.
- Convey messages or meaning using facial expression and body language.

13) Group Situations

- In a group discussion, having one person talking at a time will allow the person with dual sensory loss follow the discussion.

14) Appointment Time

● Allow additional time for meetings and appointments, as communication is slower for people who are deaf blind.

≫ 5. 8   Skills and Strategies

1) Introducing others

(1) If you have a minute, I'd like to introduce you to a good friend of mine.

(2) Ms. Gorden, I am pleased to present Algor Tang from London.

(3) Mr. Tang, I would like to introduce you to Julia Gorden, our director in charge of marketing and distribution.

(4) A busy and energetic man, but he always manages to make enough time out of his busy schedule to beat me once in a while on the golf course.

(5) She's not only fabulous with a knife, but she's also my business partner and one of my nearest and dearest friend.

(6) I am pleased to present our forest customer, Ms. Sally Friend, who will be attending our meetings throughout the day.

2) Polite questions

(1) Can you leave your name and number?

(2) Would you like to have something to drink?

(3) I'm sorry, we don't have any coffee, would tea be alright?

(4) Is there anything else I can offer you?

(5) May I please speak to George Nelson?

(6) What time are you available tomorrow for our meeting?

3) Expressing thanks

(1) I can't thank you enough for your understanding and cooperation.

(2) I really can't thank you enough for being so generous.

(3) Thank you for your hospitality.

(4) I'm grateful to you for giving me such useful advice. Your suggestions will be very helpful to me.

(5) Thank you for everything that you've done for me during my stay in China.

4) Complaints and apologies

(1) I'm so sorry for forgetting our appointment.

(2) I must apologize for making you wait for me so long.

(3) I'm sorry for being late, but I was held up in traffic for two hours.

(4) Do you mean that compared with men, women should take a lower social status?

(5) Are you laughing at me?

5) Expressing praise

(1) He has done a great job, hasn't he?

(2) Mike is the most capable person I've ever seen.

(3) You look great in your new blouse.

(4) Yon did a good job. We're so proad of you.

(5) I like the way you handled that.

<table>
<tr><td>Chapter
6</td><td></td></tr>
</table>

Business Etiquette in Dressing

In China today, people often say "clothing, food, shelter and transportation" and place "clothing" on top of the list. With the development of society, clothing does not only mean to cover up one's embarrassment or prevent one from cold, but a symbol of beauty, rank, ceremony and propriety, and most important of all, the culture carrier.

≫ 6.1 The Definition of Dressing Etiquette

Dressing etiquette refers to a kind of standard behavior in clothing, and it is the direct embody of one's social status, identity and personal taste. There are various types of dress codes.

First impressions count. A businessman who does not take the time to maintain a professional appearance presents the image of not being able to perform adequately on the job. This professional dress code is codified because many professionals have never been taught appropriate professional appearance and demeanor.

As a matter of fact, a businessman should observe standard behavior in dressing or he /she should dress different kinds of clothes on different occasions, for example, he/she should wear formal attire on attending a very formal event, or cocktail attire on having cocktails with friends.

(Skill of collocation shoes, waistband and briefcase should be in the same color; dresses from head to feet should be within three colors.)

≫ 6.2 Appearance Matters

Maybe it is unjust to judge a book by its cover, but we all do it. It is human nature. While the person in jeans may be as competent and as intelligent as the one wearing the formal suit, or more so, we do assess these attributes based on appearance. All the ingredients — knowledge, preparation, and appearance — are necessary to make a good impression.

When you work at home or in an office where casual attire is the norm, it is difficult to get out of that role and into the role of the professional in front of the audience or in front of a television camera. But, if you want to make a good impression, it is worth the effort. Here is what you need to do.

1) Please Dress Your Professional Best

Should you go out and purchase a suit for the one or two times a year you will have to make a presentation? It is probably a good idea. You should buy something classic. After all, if you are only going to wear the suit a couple of times a year, you do not want it to go out of style too quickly. Women can probably get away with a nice skirt and jacket, while men can wear dress trousers and a jacket. There is also nothing wrong with a pant suit for women. If you're going to be in front of the camera, some special rules apply. Wear neutral colors — dark blue or grey are good, don't wear large or glitzy jewelry, and wear a button down shirt or a jacket so they have somewhere to clip a microphone.

Your hair should be neat and clean. Try to keep it out of your face. As for makeup (for women out there), keep it simple. If you are going to be on camera, you should stay away from anything iridescent, frosted, or glittery.

As your mother may have told you, sit up straight. When you slouch you look bored. If you are bored, how do you expect your audience to feel? You will also look more confident if you're sitting or standing up straight. Look like you're happy to be there. Put a smile on your face. Don't fidget, bite your nails, or play with any jewelry you are wearing.

2) Your Clothes Say a Lot About You

Is it true that clothes make the man or woman? Do people form an opinion about us based on the way we dress? They do. Does that mean we should avoid any sense of individuality in the workplace? Of course not. Some types of clothing are inappropriate for certain work environments. In addition, some work environments have a dress code that all who works there must follow.

Sometimes you will not find these dress codes in writing; but if you look around you'll find that all employees are dressed in a similar way. This gives us something to think about when choosing an occupation, or a place of employment. Do we want to fit in, or do we want to be able to express our individuality on the job? The answers to these questions should play an important role in our career plans.

≫ 6.3   Basic Styles of Clothing

What is fashion? Fashion is a term commonly used to describe a style of clothing worn by most of people of a country in a certain period. A fashion usually remains popular for about one or two years and then is replaced by another fashion. So a certain style of clothing is in style one year but out of date the next. For instance, people wear sunglasses on top of their heads and wear jeans one year; however, the next year everything has changed. These names are "in" then, suddenly, these names are "out". A fashion that comes and goes fast is called a fad. A fad will not last long. Some fads disappear before we have all even heard of them. For a long-term trend or a short-term fad, certain styles and types of clothing will appear in every fashion season. Are they totally new styles? They are definitely not. Usually these latest styles are changed from some basic ones. There are a lot of changes in the length and types of sleeves, shapes of collars and innovations for some details. So to know some basic styles of clothing for us is essential.

1) Women's Wear

Clothing is something women deal with every day, even some who say they don't care what they wear. Nearly every woman attempts to express her personality and her various moods in different situations. For example, a long evening dress for a cocktail party; a blouse of sheer crept with pants or skirt for going out shopping; a knitted sweater with jeans for family reunion barbecue or a picnic. They are all suitable choices for such occasions. Women want themselves to be the most eye-catching. So choosing suitable styles of clothes is an essential skill and the most creative activity for every fashionable woman.

Let's begin with some basic styles of outwear. Outwear may be grouped under classification of occasions for which they are worn.

a. Dresses

Dresses are the most favorite outer clothing for female. They usually cover the body from shoulder to knee or below, consist of an upper bodice and a skirt section in one single piece. They are diversified in the shapes of collars, necklines and sleeves. The common styles of dress are shirt dress(the upper bodice is like a shirt with collar, concealed button closure and belted waist); coat dress (usually made of firmly fabrics with button front); princess dress(close fitting dress with long princess seams usually including 6 or 8 panels, long slim style and flared skirt); empire dress (the typical empire style is a dress with high gathered under-bust seam).

b. Skirt

Skirt is a separate garment worn and hung from the waist. It is not required to be attached to a bodice. Styles of skirts are mainly distinguished by length, width, silhouette cut and details. Skirts are various in straight skirt (slim skirt with a slight swing in the back); fared skirt (with 6-10 pieces and wider at the bottom); pleated skirt (maintain a silhouette with many tucks but free for movement); A-lined skirt(the bottom is wider than the waist and the side seam is usually in a straight line); tiered skirt (it has horizontal panels, 2, 3 or move levels and increases in width to the bottom); frilled hemline skirt(has a lower section and is with frill-paneled).

c. Pants

Women's pants are made in many styles; high-waisted, natural-waisted or low-waisted. They may fit snugly or loosely. The fashion outlines of pant legs constantly alter from classic shapes such as straight, flared, tapered pants to fashionable variations hip huggers, culottes, leggings, etc.

d. Tops

Tops that can match pants and skirts include shirts, blouses, sweaters, suit-type jackets, blazers, coats and cardigans and chemise. Some of them are typical for female, some for both sexes. Each of the types is various because of the changeable shapes of sleeves, collars and necklines. So a boy-like figure was admired and a collarless cardigan style was popular about 10 years ago but nowadays a close-fitting suit is "in".

2) Men's Wear

Men are not as picky about clothing as women and teens are. Men prefer to be comfortable, usually dress in suits or jeans, sweaters and shirts. Men like wearing plain sweaters with no pockets, or other designs. The most important styles of men's wear are formal clothes even many casual men don't like their confines. Such confining clothes include business suit, swallow-tailed coat, vest, tailored jacket, and so on

a. Business Suit

Business suit commonly has two typical types: double-breasted suit and single-breasted suit. It is for some formal occasions as making an appointment with clients, negotiating with business fellowship or signing contract.

b. Swallow-tailed Coat

Swallow-tailed coat is a type of formal attire, also called tuxedo. It is for daytime or evening party. The very formal one is black tail coat which has tails on the back cut from the side seams. The front panel is waist length, and has silk strips. It is worn with waistcoat, a shirt and a white bow-tie.

c. Tailored Jackets

Tailored jackets are made of fine suiting fabric to ensure their smooth and flat shape. They allow outfits to be put together according to individual tastes.

d. Vest

Vest is short clothes usually without covering for arms, and is worn under a suit, especially by man as part of a suit on special occasions.

≫ 6.4   Fashion Accessories

Accessories now include what many people think of — all the latest wearable things. Even top hairstylist designer's haircuts, cosmetic techniques are now considered different kinds of personal accessories. But the average accessories might simply choose from the latest style of belts, shoes, sunglasses, scarves, watches or jewelry.

1) Role of Accessories

A total look is always helpful because accessories can contribute not only to the communication of fashion theme, but also convey the type of person who would wear the "look".

Some specialists make accessories either by design or inspiration. Hats, trimmings, buttons, belts, costume jewelry, shoes and innovative pieces are finely crafted to complement the fabrics and fashion ideas. Fashion accessories are items apart from garment itself, which complement the whole outfit. They can add details to an outfit when garment's style is plain, or when the fabric has no interest. Throughout history, the world's most fashionable people have understood the power of the accessories. And fashion accessories tend to be both extremely trendy and deeply personal.

2) Head Wear

Hats have always combined fashion with practicality, offering protection from both the summer sun and the winter cold. But right now hats are experiencing a boom in popularity that has made them essential items regardless of the season. More and more people are wearing hats of distinctive designs, unlike in past hat booms, and not constrained by fashion trends. So distinguish styles of hats and caps are essential for the stylish people to match their typical clothes.

Here are some basic styles of hats and caps: berets, dress felt hats, silk hats, winter season cloth hats, western hats and straw hats.

3) Scarves

Scarves are necessities for both young and old. Great scarves are an instant way to add extra dynamic fashion color that can jazz up or soften a more somber outfit. People can also wear them as a belt, as a hair accessory or cover up a doubtful neckline to make them creative and unconventional. Finding a glamorous scarf is not difficult, but choosing from the huge variety available can be bewildering. And choosing a scarf in a ravishing material could enhance wonderful complexion color.

4) Foot Wear

Most people are capable for matching shoes and accessories with clothing in an outfit — it can often help to emphasize and complement a color or feature that might look out of place or too bold. The most important elements of foot wear are shoes, socks, stockings, etc. , shoes have varieties of types, high heel shoes, and dress shoes for women. Flat shoes, sandals, tennis shoes, loafers (casual shoes) and athletic shoes are commonly for both men and women. Choosing suitable shoes to match one's outfit might be a bread-and-butter skill for a man and a woman. For example, casual shoes and athletic shoes would be perfect with Capri pants for a long day of walking. But to wear high boots with dark hose or tights, and a short, straight skirt that hits above the knee is another different option.

5) Jewelry

Necklace: It is possible for ladies to lengthen the neck, hide flaws and even "balance out" the shape of facial region by choosing the right necklace to match one's shape and outfit. The best recommendation is to look for necklaces that give a V shape neckline. Try to go for necklaces that are in proportion to your body size and outfit. The same goes for other accessories too.

Earrings: They immediately give any women or young ladies a more sophisticated appearance. Earrings add vibrancy and can enhance your facial features. Women like wear earrings and a bracelet to work and on weekends.

6) Other Accessories

Handbags and purses are important for regular, weekend and special occasions. These items are so realistically priced that you must have one that is in great quality and will last 2-3 seasons.

Belts help define your style and finish your look, so make the most of them! All fashion styles are available right now from waist, hip through to loop styles.

Some accessories like flower corsages or charm pins are very inexpensive, but provide an instant update. You don't even have to wear corsage or scarves in traditional ways; just fix them to your handbag for an immediate fashion reviver.

After learning all the accessories, people can match their outfit more confidently with these knowledge and technologies and make you a trendy person.

≫ 6.5   Business Clothing Etiquette

Your clothing says a lot about you. How you dress for work is important. Unless your job requires you to wear a uniform, choosing clothing for work can be difficult. Of course there are industry standards, such as the navy blue suit for accountants and bankers. What do you wear, however, if you work in an industry where there really isn't a typical style of dress? Complicating the matter further are companies that allow more casual attire. How do you keep from crossing over the line from casual to sloppy? What about the job interview? You want to look your professional best, but you also want to appear as if you "fit in". Here are some pointers for dressing for any type of work situation:

● First and foremost, no matter what you wear, your clothes should be neat and clean.
● Keep your shoes in good condition.
● Your hair should be neatly styled.
● For women: makeup should be subtle.

● Nails should be clean and neat and of reasonable length.
● Dress for the job you want.

1) For Supervisors

● If your organization has no dress code, establish one.
● If your organization has one, enforce it.
● Set the standard by being compliant yourself.
● You are your employees' supervisors, not their pals. Speak up when your sensibilities are assaulted.
If all else fails, send employees home who are inappropriately dressed for your workplace.

2) For Employees

● Know your organization's dress policy.
● When in doubt, stray on the side of conservatism.
● If you hope to advance in your organization, emulate the style of those whose positions you would like to have.
● If you expect to be treated professionally, look professional—even on "Casual Friday".
● Use common sense and realize that the media sell trends and not necessarily good taste.

3) Rules for Casual Dress at Work

Although in theory most people love the idea of not having to wear a suit to work, they are often confused by the casual dress policies some employers have instituted over the last few years. Here are some simple rules:
● Casual doesn't mean sloppy. Your clothing should still be neat and clean.
● You can't go wrong with khakis and a sport shirt or a nice sweater.
● If you are going to a meeting or making a presentation, professional attire may be in order.

Obviously the standards will vary from one workplace to another. If you work for an organization that requires wearing a uniform, you can quit reading now. If you work for a business that is nontraditional and rather laissez-faire where work attire is concerned, you can stop too. For the rest of you who work in places that have established rules that can be misinterpreted or pushed to the limits, stop and look in the mirror before you leave home. Ask yourself: Does what I have to reflect the image my business wants its clients or customers to see?

≫ 6. 6 Professional Dress Code

First impressions count. A professional consultant who doesn't take the time to maintain a professional appearance presents the image of not being able to perform adequately on the job. This professional dress code is codified because many professionals have never been taught appropriate professional appearance and demeanor.

Professional dress code standards are alive-and-well in major financial and executive management and anyone who aspires to top management knows that your personal appearance counts.

If you look and behave like a highly-trained and well-groomed professional you will win the respect and honor of our valued clients.

A fresh haircut, spit-shined shoes and a crisp suit go a long way in establishing a professional demeanor.

It is also about quality; most professionals can spot a cheap suit at twenty paces and high-quality dress shoes are de-rigueur.

If you have never worked in a professional environment and you are not sure how professionals look, watch the lawyers on an episode of Law & Order on television.

1) Dress Requirement for Male Consultants

Body Art: Of course, tattoos are considered unprofessional, low-class and ignorant , and at no time may a consultant have a visible tattoo. Read details about why most corporations prohibit tattoos.

Suit: A suit means a SUIT, sport coats and slacks are not allowed. The suit must be dark blue, gray or charcoal, (except for tropical engagements) be "well tailored", and have no loose threads, "pills" or "nurdles".

Shirt: A crisp white shirt is always required. French cuffs are optional. I have seen consultants turned away at the door of banks because of their hot pink dress shirt.

Tie: Must be conservative, something a bank VP might wear.

Shoes: High-quality black lace-up shoes are required, polished to a mirror-quality spit-shine. You would be surprised at how many people judge you by your shoes.

Accessories: No phony Rolexes, body piercing or earrings.

Grooming: All hair, moustaches and beards must be neatly groomed and cologne must be used sparingly. Protruding nasal hair is prohibited and all tattoos must be fully hidden. If you have been working all-night and have an early morning meeting, you can use an anti-inflammatory hemorrhoid cream to quickly shrink those unsightly puffy bags under your eyes. Just carefully dab the cream on your lower eyelids (being careful not to get any in your eyes) and you will look fresh and well-rested.

Cologne: Cologne and after-shave is optional, but if it is used it must not be too strong as to call attention to yourself in a closed elevator.

If the client wants you to wear tattered cut-offs, that's fine, just make sure that you check with the client first to ensure that you are not dressed inappropriately for their environment

2) Dress Requirements for Female Consultants

Skirt Suit: No pants allowed, ever. The suit must be dark blue, gray or charcoal.

Blouse: A crisp white blouse is great, and you may have ruffles and other decorations.

Tie: Optional, but it must be conservative.

Shoes: High-quality black or brown shoes are required, polished to a high shine.

Jewelry: Ostentatious jewelry, multiple ear rings on each ear, and multiple chain necklaces are prohibited. Leave the Zircons at home; most people can recognize them instantly.

Cosmetics: Do not use the ski-slope approach to cosmetics (that's 3-inches of powder on top of a 6-inch base). Use no "cheap" perfumes and make sure that you do not offend allergic people with too much perfume odor.

Grooming: All hair must be neatly groomed. Females with facial hair are required to shave before any on-site engagements. You should always shave legs (if wearing skirts) and exposed armpits.

Perfume: Too much perfume is considered especially heinous when the stench is so strong as to cause allergic reactions or when the odor can be detected from more than 3 feet away. Remember, the quality of perfume is inversely proportional to the price, and many female executives can quickly tell if you are wearing a cheap, "stink pretty" perfume.

≫ 6. 7   Some Tips for Business Dressing Etiquette

Keep it simple and sophisticated is the well-known KISS principles in business circle.

People, in particular, the businessmen always want their confidence to come from their professionals' abilities, but still their clothes are important. If they dress with their next position in mind, they are more likely to get there.

It is advisable for businessmen/women to memorize these colors:

◆ Navy   ◆ Charcoal Gray   ◆ Black   ◆ Khaki   ◆ White

These are the staple colors of every business wardrobe. Here are some guidelines for both men and women to keep in mind:

1) In the Suit World, Start with the Basics

A navy blue wool suit and a charcoal wool suit, white shirts, black shoes, black belt, and black leather briefcase/notebook computer case.

2) In the Casual World, Start with the Basics

Khaki pants or skirts, white shirts, black or brown shoes and belt, and a black or brown leather and ballistic nylon briefcase/notebook computer case.

3) Add Your Own Touches in Keeping with Your Company's Style

Keep the KISS principle in mind even with casual clothes: "Keep It Simple and Sophisticated." Dark colors convey authority; bright colors convey friendliness. Light colors such as taupe and khaki are generally more casual than black, gray, or navy.

4) Try to Avoid These Fashion Mistakes

● Avoid excessive use of bright color and wild patterns.
● Avoid excessive jewelry and jewelry that signals your arrival with tiny clicking sounds.
● Your shoes do not need to "match" your blouse.
● Spiky, strappy, sandals in metallic colors or with rhinestones aren't appropriate for most businesses. Nor are open-toed shoes.
● Casual does not mean you can wear jeans. Jeans are a definite no-no in the corporate workplace unless stated otherwise in your company's dress code.

≫ 6.8   Skills and Strategies

1) Dressing for business

(1) We must wear white shirts, dark suits, and ties.
(2) Marketing and sales staff always dress for success.
(3) If you go on a sales call, you should dress formally.
(4) People judge you by your appearance, whether you like it or not.
(5) You can't go out on a sales call if you dressed in jeans because it's just not respectful to your clients.
(6) This tailored pantsuits is perfect for formal meetings.

2) Dressing for work

(1) A see-through lace top is sexy, but it's not appropriate for office wear.
(2) What should I put on if I want to look professional without wearing a suit?
(3) You may consider wearing black pantsuits often. They coordinate with most tops.
(4) If you want to have a sleek look, don't wear too many accessories.
(5) Black and off-white crew neck sweaters are always the safest choice for tops.

3) Dressing casual

(1) Neat and comfortable are the most important principles.

(2) To dress casual doesn't mean to be sloppy.

(3) We are allowed to wear more casual jackets and trousers.

(4) In some industries, there isn't such a large division between home and office, so people want to work in the clothes they feel most relaxed in.

(5) It's not necessary for you to dress up like this for shopping. If you prefer skirts, I'd say one-piece dresses and A-line skirts are good choices. You could choose a pair of flat-heeled shoes to go with you outfit.

(6) Don't wear anything that makes you feel uncomfortable.

4) Dressing for party

(1) You can try a slightly more revealing style for this party.

(2) Pulling your hair back in a neat bun is always a safe option for a formal party.

(3) This outfit is not appropriate. It's way too provocative.

(4) Your outfit is too busy and distracting.

(5) How about this pearl pink evening gown? It's very classy.

(6) Do you think this pantsuit is appropriate for a black tie party?

5) Applying makeup

(1) My complexion is a little dark. What is the best color foundation I should use?

(2) I have oily skin, what is the best way to keep makeup on?

(3) I have high cheekbones. How can I draw people's attention away from them?

(4) I have really dark circles under my eyes. How can I conceal them?

(5) My forehead is too narrow. How can I make my face look slender

(6) You can apply some blush to your cheeks. It'll brighten your face.

6) Getting facials

(1) I feel that my face is getting dehydrated, should I try the "cucumber masque"?

(2) When you apply the mask to my face, would you also apply it to my neck?

(3) You have sensitive skin, so don't exfoliate your face too often.

(4) I need to have a facial to relax a little bit.

(5) My skin looks so dull, what kind of facial treatment will improve it?

(6) My eyes look puffy. Is there a special facial that can get rid of?

(7) A professional consultant who takes the time to maintain a professional appearance presents the image of not being able to perform adequately on the job.

Chapter 7

Business Etiquette
in Dining

Business etiquette in dining has always played an important part in making a favorable impression, and in today's International Business World it has become very important to be able to project your knowledge and experience, if not your status and education, through the visible signals of the state of your manners when dining in a formal or business situation. Your actions at the table and while eating therefore, can be essential to how others perceive you and can even affect your professional success in the Business World.

≫ 7. 1　Business Dining Etiquette

Business dining etiquette refers to a series of rules and suggestions for behavior which are designed to ensure that businessmen behave consistently and with the norms of politeness. It is also an area of etiquette which pertains to dining.

Dining etiquette may vary from one culture to another which may have different norms when it comes to acceptable behavior at the table. Dining etiquette can reflect a wide variety of issues that can come up at the table. One of them is personal hygiene, an issue in a setting where people are eating because they could potentially pass diseases on to each other. Another is accepted rules of behavior when it comes to things like conversation, greeting people at the table, interacting with servers, and conversing with other diners. Other rules include how and when to use utensils and tools, from finger bowls to forks.

In some countries, food can be eaten with hands, and a complex set of rules dictates how to behave at the dinner to avoid upsetting or offending people. Other countries may use silverware or chopstick, each of which is accompanied by an assortment of etiquette rules or behavior which can vary by nation and utensil.

>>> 7. 2   Attending a Business Dinner

The most common mistake made by those people who are unaccustomed to attending formal and business functions, or are not schooled in the standard of behavior expected by those who are, most often happens immediately upon their arrival and even before the actual commencement of the event itself.

If you are attending a formal event with an escort and there is the need to remove outer clothing, capes, overcoats or raincoats, there is an accepted procedure that must be followed.

If there is a coat check attendant or a footman, then the proper procedure is for the gentleman to first hand his hat, (which should have been removed before he entered the foyer), along with his gloves and umbrella (rolled and buttoned), if he is carrying one, to the attendant.

The gentleman should always assist the lady he is escorting in removing her outer wear and pass it to the attendant, prior to removing his own. The attendant or footman is not expected to assist you, she or he is merely expected to take your clothing from you and have it stored and you should hand it to them in a folding manner, making the taking of it all the easier for the attendant. You will normally be given a ticket to retrieve your clothing after the event, which the gentleman should hold. It is also the duty of the gentleman to retrieve the clothing at the end of the function and assist the lady in dressing, before putting his own outer clothes back on.

A gentleman should nod his head slightly as he greets his host. The gentleman should then introduce his escort to the host or guest of honor, the words usually being something like: "*Mr. Ambassador, (or Sir, or Madam, or whatever is the appropriate title to use in the greeting) I would like to introduce my wife (or fiancé, escort, daughter, etc.)*". *Never* use the term "girlfriend" when introducing a lady formally. His lady should extend her hand, palm down, fingers slightly crooked and should look directly into the eyes of a male host as she is greeted (actually it is less embarrassing to look at a spot slightly above his eyes on his forehead). A lady drops her eyes when greeting her hostess.

Do not try to start a conversation, or ask a question, at the formal reception by your host, and if you are asked a question, keep the answer as short as you can and move along as fast as is polite to do, to allow those following you to be greeted. After the greeting move away, never stand around in a formal greeting area, it will only inform others that you rarely attend such events.

At most formal functions there will be a waiting room or waiting area, where the guests will gather to await the call to lunch or dinner, or to take their seats. The most blatant bad manners is to leave one's escort during this time, and this time is usually used by most guests to visit a restroom, if so then the gentleman should be waiting outside the ladies restroom for his partner to escort her back to the waiting room. It is absolutely the worst bad manners to allow your partner, male or female, to stand alone in the waiting room or waiting area while you visit the restroom.

≫ 7.3   Taking Your Seat at a Formal Dinner

Never take your seat before being invited to do so by your host. If there are not place cards to show you where the host wants you to sit, choose the seats you wish to occupy before being called to the table and stay close enough to them to be able to take them without finding yourself playing musical chairs with other guests.

If you do have the choice of seats at a large table, the best seats for a formal luncheon or dinner (once actually called the "*safe*" seats in diplomatic circles) are those that are two thirds down the table from where the host will sit, on the left side of the table as the host sees it. You will that way be served each course sooner and if introductions are called for, you will not be called upon until several others have had the chance to speak before you and inform you of the tone of the event. Never stand for the introductions — one only stands for a toast.

At most formal functions the seating is arranged so that each gentleman's lady is seated to his left and if the seating is left to the guests' choice, a gentleman should follow normal procedure and always attempt to seat his lady escort to his left.

The gentleman should always help his lady escort be seated. If you have never done this at a formal function practice with your escort before you go, if you can. Sometimes the waiters and servers will do it for you, but it is better that the gentleman himself help his escort. A gentleman is also expected to assist any unescorted lady sitting next to him to be seated. The easiest way to do this is to grasp the chair with one hand on either side of the chair back, about half-way down with your thumbs away from you. Lift the chair back so that the lady with you can walk upright to stand before the table. Then *gently* place the chair forward until the front of the seat touches your escort's legs behind the knee. Then place the chair down and your escort can sit. The lady should be standing with her torso actually touching the table before you begin this maneuver. The gentleman should stay behind the chair to assist the lady to move the chair forward. She should place one hand either side of the seat, lifting it as she moves forward, with the gentleman assisting her. The gentleman then should seat himself, once seated the gentleman should also adjust the position of his chair with one hand on either side of the seat.

Most men have been told by their mother that they should always help a lady be seated, but from observation it would appear that many mothers often forget to tell their sons that a gentleman also is expected to assist a lady when she needs to leave her seat at the end of a meal. In fact if she is wearing a long dress or a ball gown, she needs the help to get up far more after the meal is over than she needed the help to sit down initially.

At the end of the meal, a gentleman lifts his chair back with his hands grasping the seat of his chair and then moves to stand directly behind his escort's chair to be able to assist her stand. Taking the chair in exactly the same manner as he placed it beneath her for her to sit down, he waits for her to begin to rise and then pulls the chair back from underneath her. However, there are also ladies whose mother never told them how to rise when being helped with her chair by a gentleman. The easiest and the safest procedure to follow, which will prevent her from losing her balance and depositing her derriere quickly to the floor, is to move her right foot back and turn as she rises and the chair is removed from beneath her, steadying her balance by initially placing her left hand upon the table, and holding her purse with her right hand, and then exiting her place to her right between her own place and the gentleman's removed chair. Again, it is helpful if you can practice this maneuver prior to the event

≫ 7. 4   Using Napkin

The meal actually begins when the host or hostess unfolds his or her napkin. You should never attempt to call the waiters or other staff to assist you before the meal begins. When the host has opened his or her napkin this is the guest's signal to do the same. The gentleman should pick up his escort's napkin with his right hand, take it by a corner and shake it open beneath the table level to the right of his chair. He should then lay it upon his escort's lap, still holding only the corner and only using his right hand, so that she may adjust it, and then he should take his own napkin and repeat the procedure for himself.

Lifting a table napkin occasionally is made difficult by the way it has been folded before being placed upon the table. The following guide will allow you to properly open the napkin. You take the napkin off the table with your right hand only, taking the "*opening point*" between your forefinger and thumb and it should begin to fall open as you move it from the table. The name beneath each illustration is the professional description of the type of folding.

Place your napkin on your lap, completely unfolded if it is a small luncheon napkin, or in half diagonally, across your lap point at your knees, if it is a large dinner napkin. Never tuck the napkin into any part of your clothing or remove it during the meal, unless you are called upon to stand for a toast. In that case, fold your napkin neatly and place it to the left of your plate before standing, and do not forget to return it to your lap when retaking your seat. After a toast is the only time a lady would remove her napkin from the table herself and replace it on her lap. Typically, you want to put your napkin on your lap soon after sitting down at the table (but follow your host's lead). The napkin remains on your lap throughout the meal and should you need to, and after each course without fail, it should be used to gently blot your mouth.

Never wipe your silverware with your napkin. If you should drop a utensil, or one is not absolutely clean, call a waiter or server to assist you and have it replaced. If you need to leave the table during the meal, fold your napkin twice and place it over the back of your chair.

Host will signal the end of the meal by placing his or her napkin on the table. Once the meal is over, you too should place your napkin neatly folded on the table to the left of your plate.

≫ 7. 5   Choosing the Right Silverware

Choosing the correct silverware from the variety in front of you is really not as difficult as it may at first appear, if you know the basic approach to laying a table. The golden rule is *"from the outside in"* , to be more exactly, just starting with the knife, fork, or spoon that is farthest from your plate, work your way in, using a new utensil or set of them, for each course. Americans often only use the salad fork to eat their salad, thereby ignoring the salad knife which most American restaurants and hotels still lay beside their plate. Obviously there is nothing wrong with this if it is your preference; however, when you have finished eating your salad it shows knowledge to lay the salad knife upon the plate beside the fork to signal to the waiter that you have finished.

At a four course formal dinner, your soup spoon will be on your outermost right, followed by your salad knife, a fish knife and then the dinner knife. Your salad fork will be on your outermost left, then your fish fork and your dinner fork will be nearest your plate. Your dessert spoon and fork will usually be laid above your plate in America or brought out with the dessert. In Europe at the better establishments and at State Functions your desert spoon and fork will actually be laid on either side, and nearest to your plate. Sometimes a butter knife will be laid to the right of your plate, (it is a small knife with a rounded, dull blade,) but normally today it is placed upon your side plate. However, if you remember the rule to work from the outside in, or to watch what the more experienced people at your table are doing, you will be fine.

There are two ways to use a knife and fork to cut and eat your food. They are the American style and the European style. In most situations either style is considered appropriate. In the American style, one cuts the food by holding the knife in the right hand and the fork in the left hand with the fork tines holding the food to the plate. The right method is to cut a few bite-size pieces of food, then lay your knife across the top edge of your plate with the sharp edge of the blade facing inwards and towards you. Then change your fork from your left hand into your right hand to eat, with the fork tines facing up. (If you are left-handed, keep your fork in your left hand, tines facing up.) The European style is the same as the American style in that you cut your meat by holding your knife in your right hand with your forefinger pressed on the back of the blade, while securing your food with your fork held tines down in your left hand. Your fork remains in your left hand however, and good manners dictate that at all times the tines must be facing down. The knife must always stay in your right hand, and not be put down while eating, except when you need your right hand to lift your wine glass. The food is then either taken by pushing the fork into it, or by pushing the food onto the back of the fork with your knife. The fork is never used in a shoveling motion in the European style as it often is in the American style.

≫ 7.6 When You Have Finished Eating

After each course you should lightly dab your mouth with your napkin and wipe the corners of your mouth, using your right hand to lift a corner only of the napkin to your face to do so.

Never push your plate away from you when you are finished eating, or move it aside. Leave your plate where it is and it will be collected by your waiter.

Never try to help your waiter, or attempt to hand him or her a plate that you have finished with, merely lean to one side (most often you will lean to the right for food to be served or taken away, and to the left,) when drinks are served or glasses are removed.

The most common way to inform the waiter that you are finished with a course of the meal is to lay your fork and knife together across your plate. Place your knife and fork side by side, with the sharp side of the knife blade facing inward and the fork, tines up, to the left of the knife with both of the handles nearest to you. Make sure that they are placed so that they touch each other and that they will not slide off the plate as it is removed.

Once you have used a piece of silverware, never place it back on the table. Do not leave a used spoon in a cup either; place it on the saucer. You also leave a soup spoon in a soup plate when you have finished eating, bowl facing upwards and with the handle again nearest to you.

≫ 7.7 Chinese Dining Etiquette

Chinese appreciate foreigners' efforts to eat with chopsticks. If using chopsticks proves impossible and no forks are available, you can use the porcelain spoon.

Formal banquets often include a dozen or more dishes. While declining to taste a dish is not considered a cardinal offense, it is polite to try each dish that is served. This means it is important to pace yourself. Leaving a little on your plate signals your Chinese host that you are full. This is also a good strategy to avoid receiving another serving of a dish you do not like. An empty plate is a cue to your Chinese host that you are still hungry, and it will likely continue to be filled until you leave something on it.

According to Chinese custom it is the role of the host to serve food to their guests, so do not be surprised if the host places food on your plate. If you are feeling very polite and have good chopstick control, you may reciprocate and attempt to serve the host, but it is not necessary. If you are hosting a dinner or banquet it is polite to make a gesture of serving guests on either side and then state clearly that everyone should please help himself/herself, adding "we are all friends and should be informal".

≫ 7. 8   Good Manners at the Table

Table manners play an important part in making a favorable impression. They are visible signals of the state of our manners and therefore are essential to professional success. Regardless of whether we are having lunch with a prospective employer or dinner with a business associate, our manners can speak volumes about us as professionals. Some tips are offered as follows:

● If you don't like what's being served, don't say so. Just keep quiet and let it sit. Place your spoon or fork on the plate (if soup, on the soup plate, not in the soup).

● Never use your fingers at any formal dining experience, (except for moving pieces of bread to your mouth) unless a delicacy is served which it is impossible to eat unless one uses one's fingers.

● Don't put your used napkin on the top of the table. Leave it on your seat where no one has to look at it.

● When confronted with a place setting of three or four forks and spoons that confuses you, a good rule of thumb is to start with the outermost utensil and work your way in with each course. In general the dishes for liquids are the right, while dishes for solids are on the left.

● Cut only two to three pieces of meat at a time. Resist the temptation to cut up the whole thing all at once.

● Signal the servers that you are still eating by pacing your fork and knife in an inverted V on your plate from the 10 to 4 o'clock positions.

● Don't season your food before you have tasted it, or it is an insult to the Chef who prepared the meal and thereby it is also an insult to your host.

● Never chew with your mouth open, or make loud noises when you eat. A polite person *always* closes their mouth while eating.

● Don't ask the waiter for a "*doggy bag*" to take home the leftovers when you are a guest at either a formal function or at a good restaurant. If the waiter suggests you can take home the leftovers, decline with a polite but firm, "*Thank you, but no*".

● When you are not eating, keep your hands in your lap, or resting on the table (with only your wrists on the edge of the table). An elbow placed upon the table is completely unacceptable in polite company.

● Never leave the table during a meal except in an emergency. If you must go to the restroom, or if you suddenly become sick, tell your escort and quietly excuse yourself to your immediate neighbors only. Later you can apologize to the host by saying that you did not feel well, but try to interrupt the event as little as possible.

● Turn cell phones off when you are attending a formal or business function. If you must have cell phone access, use the vibrator or voice mail options so you don't disturb those sitting with you or around you.

● If you need something that you cannot reach easily at the table, call the waiter and quietly ask for it to be brought to you. You should never rise from your chair to reach for something during a formal dining experience.

● If food spills off your plate, use your silverware to pick it up and place it on the right hand side of your plate.

● Never spit anything into your napkin. Remove gristle or fat, or other unwanted food from your mouth using the same utensil you used to put it in your mouth if you can. If that is not possible, cover your mouth with your left hand and remove it with your right hand. Place the piece of food on the edge of your plate and, if possible, cover it with some other food, so that other guests do not have to look at it while they are eating.

≫ 7.9 Skills and Strategies

1) Making an invitation

(1) Would you stay for dinner, please?

(2) Will you have dinner with us?

(3) Would you like something to eat?

(4) We're giving a buffet dinner in honor of the New York Trade Delegation at 6:30 at Great Wall Hotel this evening. Would you like to join us?

(5) My we have the pleasure of inviting you to join us to have dinner at Garden Hotel at 7 tomorrow?

(6) Please ask your wife to join us for dinner tonight.

2) Accepting an invitation

(1) That's very kind of you. I'd be delighted to come.

(2) We're at your disposal.

(3) Thank you. It's thoughtful of you. I think she would be glad to go with me.

(4) Yes, with pleasure.

(5) Yes, I'd like to very much.

(6) Yes, that sounds nice/lovely/terrific.

3) Drinking toasts

(1) To your health! / Here's looking at you!

(2) To the success of our cooperation.

(3) Cheers! / Drink up! / To bottoms up!

(4) May I propose a toast to our friendship and friendly cooperation?

(5) I'd like to propose a toast to our distinguished British guests.

(6) To our host's health, and to the health of all the gentlemen present.

4) During the banquet

(1) I'd like to propose a toast.

(2) Make yourself at home. /Don't stand on ceremony.

(3) This is a toast for Mr. Anderson.

(4) May I help you to some sweet and sour pork?

(6) I'm glad you enjoy Chinese food, hope the dishes will give you a better idea of Chinese cooking.

5) Commenting on dishes

(1) The roast duck is a Beijing specialty. Please help yourself.

(2) This dish is really attractive and appetizing.

(3) Sichuan food is very delicious. I see your cook takes care of the color, flavor and taste all at the same time.

(4) The beef is too tough and fish is too raw.

(5) The soup is heavily seasoned.

(6) This dish tastes kind of salty/sour/greasy/stale.

6) Explaining the ways of cooking

(1) Slice the duck, add the chopped garlic and serve with the sauce.

(2) Bring the water to boil and boil the chicken for about 15 minutes.

(3) Simmer the spare ribs over low heat for half an hour.

(4) Mix the minced pork with the chopped cabbage, garlic and onion, and add a spoonful ofsugar, a little salt, a bit of gourmet powder and pepper.

(5) Marinate the fish in cooking wine and soy sauce for ten minutes, then sprinkle salt and white pepper on it.

(6) Slice the cucumbers and put the slices in a bowl, then add some vinegar and sugar.

(7) Stir-fry the beef with celery for about 5 minutes.

(8) Steam the fish in the microwave oven for 5 minutes.

7) Talking about cooking

(1) Chinese food is characterized by its color, aroma and flavor.

(2) In general, in addition to flavors, Chinese cuisine gives special attention to the food's nutrition, colors and textures.

(3) Guangdong, Sichuan, Shandong and Jiansu cuisine are the four most famous Chinese cuisine.

(4) Jiangsu cuisine is famous for its wide variety of ingredients and sweetish flavors.

(5) Cantonese cuisine is known for raw, lightly-cooked foods preserving the original flavors.

(6) Sichuan cuisine is noted for its hot and spicy flavors.

(7) Shandong cooking is characterized by its seafood dishes.

8) After the banquet

(1) Thank you for having us.

(2) Thanks a lot for having us.

(3) I had a lovely time.

(4) Thank you for a lovely evening.

<table>
<tr><td>Chapter
8</td><td></td></tr>
</table>

Business Etiquette in Interview

Good manners are very important and can often determine whether or not you get the job. The atmosphere in the corporate job world is so much different from that in typical college jobs; once you're hired after college, you're expected to know how to dress and act.

≫ 8.1 The Definition of Interview Etiquette

According to company recruiters and hiring managers nationwide, proper etiquette among students they've interviewed is sorely lacking. Companies not only want strong academic credentials and solid leadership skills, they're also insisting on excellent interpersonal skills and etiquette is considered a component of those skills. Employers can afford to be very choosy in who they hire due to the challenging job market, so get a head start on the competition. The common etiquettes that one should take into consideration in their job-hunting are listed as follows:

1) Scrutinize Your Writing

You should proofread and edit your resume/cover letters; have someone review them.

2) Dress Appropriately for Each Company and Industry

You have to be aware of dress requirements for each company; dressing professionally will help you develop self-confidence as well as gain the confidence of others. You'd better get something to read on dressing for an interview, or a video regarding dress and etiquette.

3) Show Genuine Enthusiasm

You should be natural; people respond well to this. Get excited about the job you're interviewing for — express interest.

4) Be Patient

Not everything that is faster is necessarily better; learn to differentiate between being appropriately persistent and immaturely impatient.

5) Watch What You Say and How Long You Take to Say It

This ranges from how you address others to avoiding slang expressions such as, "you know" or "like"; an intelligent response to an interview question should be between 2 and 6 sentences, not 6 paragraphs or 6 words.

6) Learn to Listen

Listening is an essential tool for several reasons: by listening to others, you flatter them by showing that what they're saying is important; also, by listening you're learning and increasing your chances of succeeding — how will you understand what your responsibilities are if you're not listening?

7) Always Be Ready to Demonstrate What You Can Do to Help

It is your job to know what you can do; emphasize what you can do for the company, not what the company can do for you.

8) Know How to Eat Properly

Proper table manners are expected. Table manners play an important part in making a favorable impression. They are visible signals of the state of our manners and therefore are essential to professional success.

9) Be on Time

Timeliness is a must, plan to leave and extra 10 minutes earlier than normal. Timeliness contributes to your chances of success.

10) Adopt a Friendly Attitude

Believe in yourself; smiling is never out of style! Be remembered as a nice person who appears happy, relaxed, and interested in others and easy with which to work.

Etiquette involves concentrating on being polite, warm, and friendly and being graceful with your body. Be yourself, not someone else. Good manners will get you where you're going faster than a speeding BMW!

≫ 8. 2　Etiquette for Business Interview

Interviews are often stressful — even for job seekers who have interviewed many times. Interviewing can be even more stressful when you are expected to eat and talk at the same time.

One of the reasons employers take job candidates out to lunch or dinner is to evaluate their social skills and to see if they can handle themselves gracefully under pressure.

Dining with a prospective employee allows employers to review your communication and interpersonal skills, as well as your table manners, in a more relaxed (for them) environment. Table manners do matter. Good manners may give you the edge over another candidate, so, take some time to brush up your dining etiquette skills.

1) Interview Dining Tips:

● Are you really nervous? Check out the restaurant ahead of time. That way you'll know exactly what's on the menu, what you might want to order and where the rest rooms are located.

● Be polite. Remember to say "please" and "thank you" to your server as well as to your host.

● Is the table full of utensils? My British grandmother taught me an easy way to remember what to use when. Start at the outside and work your way in. Your salad fork will be on the far left; your entree fork will be next to it. Your dessert spoon and fork will be above your plate.

● Liquids are on the right, solids on the left. For example, your water glass will be on the right and your bread plate will be on the left.

● Put your napkin on your lap once everyone is seated.

● Remember what your mother spent years telling you: keep your elbows off the table, sit up straight, and don't talk with your mouth full!

2) During the Meal

● Don't order messy food — pasta with lots of sauce, chicken with bones, ribs, big sandwiches, and whole lobsters are all dangerous.

● Don't order the most expensive entree on the menu.

● Do order food that is easy to cut into bite-size pieces.

● The polite way to eat soup is to spoon it away from you. There's less chance of spilling in your lap that way too!

● Break your dinner roll into small pieces and eat it a piece at a time.

● If you need to leave the table, put your napkin on the seat or the arm of your chair.

● When you've finished eating, move your knife and fork to the "four o'clock" position so the server knows you're done.

● Remember to try and relax, listen, and participate in the conversation.

3) To Drink or Not to Drink

● It's wise not to drink alcohol during an interview. Interviewing is tough enough without adding alcohol to the mix.

4) After the Meal

- Put your napkin on the table next to your plate.
- Let the prospective employer pick up the tab. The person who invited you will expect to pay both the bill and the tip.
- Remember to say "thank you." Consider also following-up with a ***thank-you note*** which reiterates your interest in the job.

≫ 8.3 The Best Way to Reduce Interview Stress

Interviews are always stressful — even for job seekers who have gone on countless interviews. The best way to reduce the stress is to be prepared. Take the time to review the "standard" interview questions you will most likely be asked. Also review sample answers to these typical interview questions.

Then take the time to research the company. That way you'll be ready with knowledgeable answers for the job interview questions that specifically relate to the company you are interviewing with.

Interview questions:

- What were your expectations for the job and to what extent were they met?
- What were your starting and final levels of compensation?
- What were your responsibilities?
- What major challenges and problems did you face? How did you handle them?
- Which was most/least rewarding?
- What was the biggest accomplishment/failure in this position?
- Who was your best boss and who was the worst?
- Why are you leaving your job?
- What have you been doing since your last job?

In addition to being ready to answer these standard questions, prepare for behavior based interview questions. This is based on the premise that a candidate's past performance is the best predictor of future performance. You will you need to be prepared to provide detailed responses including specific examples of your work experiences. The best way to prepare is to think of examples where you have successfully used the skills you have acquired.

You will have to take the time to compile a list of responses to both types of interview questions and to itemize your skills, values, and interests as well as your strengths and weaknesses. You should emphasize what you can do to benefit the company rather than just what you are interested in, and have your references checked prior to getting an offer. Plan ahead and compile a list of references and some letters of recommendations now, so you're prepared when the employer requests them.

>>> 8. 4   Etiquette for a Job Interview

In addition to following the general rules for dressing for work, heed this advice when you go on a job interview:

● Adhere to the employer's dress code: find out whether it's formal (suit and tie) or casual by asking around or by observing employees arriving for work.

● Dress slightly better than you would if you were an employee. For example, if the dress code is very casual, you should take it up a notch.

● Cover up tattoos and remove body jewelry until you know whether they are acceptable at that particular workplace.

A big job interview is coming up and you are feeling very confident. You have anticipated the questions they might ask and have prepared some great answers. Fresh copies of your resume are sitting in your backpack. Wait a minute. Did you say backpack? Are you really going to walk into a job interview carrying a backpack? Next thing you'll say is that you're planning to wear jeans and a T-shirt. You better ask yourself these questions before you get dressed.

1) What Should I Wear?

Generally, it's a good idea to wear a suit for a job interview. Go with something simple, in a neutral tone. The more conservative your field is, the more conservative your suit should be. For example, if you're applying for a job in an investment firm, go with a navy blue or dark gray suit.

2) What If My Interview Is for a Job in a More Casual Setting?

It's a good idea to match your interview attire to the prospective job.

If you are applying for a job working on a warehouse floor, you will look out of place wearing a formal suit. Keeping that in mind, dress a little better than you would for a day at work and make sure your clothes are neat and clean.

3) My Interview Is for a Job in an Accounting Firm. Traditionally this Field Is Conservative, But This Particular Firm May Be a Little More Casual. How Should I Dress?

You can't go wrong in a suit, but if you want to give more of an impression of "fitting in" then you need to find out how people actually dress for work at that firm. One way to do this is to observe people arriving for work. Choose any day other than a Friday, which is when some companies allow more casual dress. Again, follow the rule of dressing better for the interview than you would for a typical day at the office.

4) Do I Have to Buy a New Suit?

As long as your suit is in good condition and not outdated, you don't have to buy a new one. If you do decide to purchase a new suit, buy the best one you can afford and make sure you don't get anything too trendy. You want your investment to last.

5) What Shoes Should I Wear?

In all instances, wear closed-toe shoes. Sandals are never appropriate for a job interview, unless you are applying for a job as a lifeguard. Black shoes match everything (yes, even your navy blue suit). Stick with a conservative style. Women should not wear very high heels.

6) Must I Buy New Shoes?

No. Shoes you've already worn are fine, unless they are in bad condition or out of style. A little shoe polish may be in order here.

7) What About My Nails?

Your nails should be clean. A man's nails should be kept short and a woman's nails shouldn't be excessively long and should be bare or polished in a neutral color.

8) I Love Wearing Jewelry. Can I Wear It for the Interview?

Modest jewelry is fine, but don't wear large earrings or a thick chain.

9) What about Makeup? How Much Is OK?

Don't paint on the makeup. Keep it simple and use neutral colors.

10) What Should I Carry with Me — a Purse, a Briefcase, a Backpack?

By all means, leave the backpack at home. You want to look professional, not like you're taking a stroll across campus. A woman can carry a small to medium sized handbag. A man or woman can carry a briefcase if he or she wishes, or a folder or portfolio.

≫ 8. 5   Case Study — An Interview with Shell Oil Company

The Shell Oil Company is well-known for its human resource assessment methodology, which has proven successful in the identification and selection of candidates for its global operations. Its approach and assessment criteria have been adopted by some government agencies for selecting scholars and public officials.

The second largest global oil giant and a *Fortune* 500 company, Shell is known for its stringent selection criteria when it comes to executive hiring. The interview process of this world-class company is very thorough and demands a lot out of a candidate. The whole experience is exhausting (it lasts approximately 6 hours including lunch) and one has to be very well prepared mentally to perform well. Candidates who are further short-listed after this process will still have to go through more interviews before being hired

The setting is as such: The candidate, along with 5-6 other short-listed candidates, is invited to a local hotel/resort/country club for a day. The panel that will be interviewing you consists of senior managers from different divisions of the company.

One point to note for perspective: Through this thorough interview process, the company seeks to employ candidates who can eventually progress to a General Management position in one of the company's numerous divisions. The various stages of the long process include:

Step One: Panel Interview

Candidates are first put through an interview regarding one's personal and education background, career objectives, achievements, extra curricular activities, etc. The panel usually consists of senior management from different divisions of the company. Some of the questions asked featured in the "Frequently Asked Questions".

Step Two: Panel Discussion

Candidates discuss with the rest of the short listed candidates. The Human Resource personnel will normally chair this session. Topics are typically general in nature and the key here is to assess how each candidate engages in the discussion process, how nimble is their thought process and their grasp of current issues outside of the normal textbook environment. (Keeping silent and not engaging in the process would be an absolute disaster.)

Step Three: Lunch with the Interviewers

Though a free lunch, it comes with a purpose. This session is used to gauge the social and dinning etiquette of a candidate. How he behaves, conducts conversations over lunch, and the obvious table manners. Try not to slurp loudly and stuff yourself too full, as the afternoon sessions are even more demanding and a full stomach will only dull your thought process.

Step Four: Presentation to Interviewers and Rest of Candidates

One is asked to give a short 5 minutes speech/presentation on a topic of one's choice, and to take some questions following that. (There will definitely be some from the interviewers.) The purpose of this is to test your presentation skills and presence.

Step Five: In-Tray Exercise

Candidate is sited behind a desk and asked to review various memos, e-mails that are in his in-tray. Issues cut across the various functions, marketing, sales, finance, audit, control and human resource. The candidates were asked how they would act and why in every one of the highlighted issues. It is a vigorous and demanding exercise. They focus on how you react under the different circumstances, the decisions made on every issue and your thought process when arriving at the decision. They do not expect the candidates to have full understanding of the various operations, thus it is also a test of how one copes under pressure and in new/unfamiliar situations. (This exercise displays the "helicopter" qualities of the person, whether he has the maturity and qualities to make a good manager.)

Step Six: Cocktails

Top management would typically join the candidates and the interviewers for cocktails at the end of the day. Though it is a time to finally relax and get to know each one better, it is also an excellent opportunity to reinforce one's strengths and qualities. This is the best opportunity to make an impression on top management, thus prepare the right questions and be ready to engage.

≫ 8.6　A Good Fit with the Organization

Physical appearance is often a consideration, because clothing and grooming reveal something about a candidate's personality and awareness of industry standards. If you show up in casual clothes at Apple Computer, for example, you may be greeted as kindred spirit, but the same outfit would work against you at a conservative law firm. Apart from noticing a candidate's clothes, interviewers also size up such physical factors as posture, eye contact, handshake, facial expressions, and tone of voice.

An interviewer might also consider age in deciding whether an applicant will fit in with the organization (although job discrimination against the middle-aged is prohibited by law). If you feel your youth could count against you, counteract its influenced by emphasizing your experience, dependability, and mature attitude.

A candidate's personal background-interests, hobbies, awareness of world event, and the like — is also regarded as an indicator of how well the person will fit the organization. You can expand your potential along these lines by reading widely, making an effort to meet new people, and participating in discussion groups, seminars, and workshops.

Attitude and style are other personal qualities that employers look at. Openness, enthusiasm, and interest are likely to impress an interviewer. So are courtesy, insecurity, willingness to learn, and a positive, self-confident — all of which help a new employee adapt to a new workplace and new responsibilities.

≫ 8.7　Some Tips for a Successful Interview

Here are the pointers to get you started on a successful interview:

1) To Relax

It seems impossible but just concentrates on breathing deeply. The idea is to keep oxygen flowing to your brain so that you can remember all the reasons why you deserve this job. Deep breathing also prevents you from losing consciousness.

A display of nervousness may thwart your ability to negotiate the best deal and may even harm your chances of getting the job.

2) Be on Time

Leave a few minutes for construction delays, traffic, and a pit stop. If you have never been to this building get specific directions, including where to park, which entrance to use and where to go once you get inside. Write the information down and drive over a day or two in advance so that your getting lost would not be a delay.

3) Get the Correct Pronunciation of Your Interviewer's Name

Get the information when you ask for directions and if the name is hard to pronounce practice on it.

4) Know Your Interviewer's Title and Use It Until You Are Asked to Do Otherwise

Do not call your interviewer by their first name until you've been informed by your host that you can drop the titles and surnames.

5) Bring a Folder with a Few Clean Copies of Your Résumé

Some paper to write on, a good fountain pen with quick drying ink and a tissue or two: A leather portfolio adds a nice touch but avoid bringing too much luggage.

6) Be Polite and Patient While Waiting on Your Interviewer

It is important to make a good impression with the people that might end up being your co-workers.

On the other hand, you don't want to be overly friendly. Take your cue from the employee, if he strikes up a conversation, go with it. But if he seems busy, don't bother him.

7) Don't Chew Gum, Smoke, Eat, or Drink on Company Premises

Avoid taking even a bottle of water. During the interview:
● Start with a smile and firm handshake — obviously!
● Stand up when your interviewer approaches.
● Greet him by name, look him in the eye, and thank him for this opportunity.

● Give the interview your full attention: Minimize possible distractions by turning off pagers, cell phones, watches, and other beeping gadgets.

8) Be as Specific as Possible in Answering the Interviewer's Questions

It is always better to get the possible questions in advance (with the help of available resources) in order to get prepared for the interview. Try to use your own experiences whenever possible and always give yourself time to think before you speak.

9) Add Other Comments and Ask Questions at the End of the Interview

Avoid asking questions that can easily be answered through a website or annual report — if you ask them the interviewer may conclude that you didn't take the time to research the company.

≫　8. 8　Skills and Strategies

1) Job Interview questions about you

(1) What is your greatest weakness?

(2) What is your greatest strength?

(3) Describe a typical work week.

(4) How do you handle stress and pressure?

(5) What are your salary expectations?

(6) Do you prefer to work independently or on a team?

(7) Give some examples of teamwork.

2) Interview questions about your abilities

(1) Describe a time when your workload was heavy and how you handled it.

(2) Describe a difficult work situation / project and how you overcame it.

(3) What do you find are the most difficult decisions to make?

(4) What type of work environment do you prefer?

(5) How do you evaluate success?

(6) If you know your boss is 100% wrong about something, how would you handle it?

3) Interview questions about the new job

(1) What interests you about this job?

(2) What applicable attributes / experience do you have?

(3) Are you overqualified for this job?

(4) Why are you the best person for the job?

(5) What can you do for this company?

(6) Why should we hire you?

4) Interview questions about the company

(1) What do you know about this company?

(2) Why do you want to work here?

(3) What challenges are you looking for in a position?

(4) What can you contribute to this company?

(5) Are you willing to travel?

(6) Is there anything I haven't told you about the job or company that you would like to know?

5) Interview questions about the future

(1) What are you looking for in your next job? What is important to you?

(2) How do you plan to achieve those goals?

(3) What are your goals for the next five years / ten years?

(4) What are your salary requirements — both short-term and long-term?

(5) What will you do if you don't get this position?

Chapter 9

Business Etiquette in Negotiation

International business negotiation is a consultative process between governments, trade organizations, multinational enterprises, private business firms and buyers and sellers in relation to investment and import and export of products, machinery and equipments and technology. Negotiation is one of the important steps taken towards completing import and export trade agreements.

To reach the desired results, the negotiators must seriously carry out the relative trade policies of their own countries. They should have good manners and speak fluent English. They should have a profound knowledge of professional technology and international markets. They should know the specifications, packing, features and advantages of the products and be able to use idiomatic and professional terms. They should know something about the counterparts, such as their habits and customs in order to easily find harmony with them when negotiating business.

≫ 9.1 Some Basic Etiquette for Negotiation

In order to avoid misunderstandings and vagueness, and effectively navigate the other party through the negotiations, there is some basic etiquette that you need to keep in mind:

1) Listen Attentively, Ask Questions

Concentrate on the other party's body language. By leaning forward, making eye contact, nodding your head, and by "um-m-m-ing" and "ah-a-a-ing" you signal your interest in what the other has to say. Always listen until the other party has finished their last word rather than starting to think about your own counter argument as soon as they begin talking.

Being patient, talking less, and waiting are often the keys to a miracle. Your silence allows the other party to express their ideas which will not only make them feel as though they are being taken seriously, but will also give you time to get an overall grasp on the situation. When negotiating, you will stamina and endurance usually count the most.

Ask questions, rather than simply interpreting a statement in the way you believe to have understood it. When asking, use certain key words that the other party mentioned in their last statement.

Do not accept all problems that get sent your way, but figure out a way to send them back. Problems often are not as serious as they seem at the beginning of negotiations. Try to put "problems" aside so that you can concentrate more on goals that are practical and achievable until the heat has gone out of the argument. By the way, you should know that the word "Problem" ("problem") is frowned upon in the German business world, and it should be avoided whenever possible. Use the word "Schwierigkeit" ("difficulty") instead. This word leaves more of an impression that the situation can be solved.

2) Repeat, and Summarize

Repeat basic statements throughout the negotiation process such as, "So, I understand that to mean...". This lets others know that you are paying attention to what is being discussed and, when you express issues in your own words, you ensure that you have understood correctly. Avoid making your own interpretations, judgments or allegations. Restating a proposal or position also helps bring focus when the discussion has strayed. Repetition also has other advantages:

● If you do not want to reply to a question immediately (or at all), repetition wins you more time.
● If someone is talking too much but saying very little, repetition will allow you to capture the gist of what the person is trying to say and refocus them on the subject.
● If someone says something vague or confusing you can repeat or restate what they have said to help clarify your understanding. ("So basically, you are saying that...")
● If many different arguments are at hand, restatement allows you to prioritize the issues. ("So the most important thing for you seems to be...")

By repeating what someone has said, you often lead them to supply additional arguments. Therefore, if you want to get additional information from the other party, you may find this method useful.

Put together a summary at the end of each negotiation phase. Summarize what was agreed upon and what needs further clarification. This summary will allow you to refer to the main points of the negotiations, structure the rest of the negotiation process and provide a basis for the next discussion.

≫ 9.2   A Good Negotiator

A good negotiator is usually described as having the patience of a clockmaker and not suffering from prejudices or stereotypes. When you take part in a business negotiation, you need to keep the following pointers in mind:

First, you should make sure that you do not confront the other party immediately with arguments and demands. Take time at the beginning of the negotiations to break the ice and establish rapport. This can be achieved by discussing a non-controversial current event which might include sports, entertainment, business issues, etc. However, don't go into detail about the traffic jam on the highway, the search for a parking spot, or the bad weather — you need to save time for the "major" topics to be discussed.

Second, you'd better set up your goal and plan your negotiation time. As the saying goes, "He who does not know where he wants to go will never get there". Be sure that you go into negotiations with concrete goals in mind, based on the answers to the following questions:

● What is my most important goal?
● What is NOT negotiable?
● What are the possible trade-offs or concessions? What do I require in return?
● Where is the compromise threshold or where should I draw the line?

In order to make the threshold of possible compromises clear, you can call on a higher authority. However, be very careful when making this move, otherwise you could leave the impression that you do not possess bargaining authority. If the other party chooses to bring a higher authority into the discussion, ask them exactly what their intention is.

Many negotiators reserve a higher authority for final ratification or the approval of the tentative agreement. This empowers the negotiator to engage in meaningful discussion until the end of the negotiating process. Every negotiator must know what his limits are PRIOR to negotiations or he runs the risk of his efforts not being approved.

Also, be sure that you do not just have your own goals in mind. In order to remain reputable, you also have to consider the needs of the other party; otherwise a compromise will not be possible. A successful negotiation results in both parties getting something they value.

For example: If you ask your boss for a raise, and you cannot justify your asking by listing a few of your major accomplishments for the company or your increasing responsibilities, you are destined to fail.

In addition, before going into negotiations, it is helpful to learn what you can about the other party's interests, needs, philosophy, style and level of knowledge. This will help you to better understand the other party's position and the arguments offered. In this way, you can prepare compromises that allow you to achieve the full extent of your goals.

≫ 9.3   Some Guidelines for Successful Negotiation

In the business world, you must negotiate constantly with clients, suppliers, colleagues, and even supervisors. Consider the following 6 points, and you will be able to successfully build freedom to negotiate in your discussions with business partners and come to sound business decisions.

1) Genuinely Communicate Your Own Strengths

Make sure that you communicate your own strengths, regardless of whether others have the same strengths or not. Today's negotiation coaches recommend saying what you really think. Fixed negotiation formulas and behavior schematics are, on the contrary, no longer "in". Honesty and trustworthiness are most important because the other party will quickly see the discrepancy between verbal and nonverbal communication. If you are fuming on the inside, nobody will buy the stoic mask that you are trying to play off on the outside. For this reason, it is better to allow your feelings to come into the negotiation process when it is appropriate and in ways that are constructive.

2) Pick the Right Moment

As you prepare for your negotiations, do not just think about which arguments you plan to use, but consider which point in the negotiation process would be the best time to use them. By planning in this way, you will be able to make your arguments more potent. Timing is also important when it comes to making an appointment for the negotiations. For things that are considered to be especially important — to you, your employees or your colleagues — you should always make a separate appointment to discuss them. A serious and executable decision can seldom be made when negotiations are hurried.

3) Be Fair and Objective

When negotiating, keep cool and do not let your emotions get the best of you. If your proposal or position leaves the other party annoyed, do not consider this to be a sign of success. In fact, this usually means you have put a barrier in the way of a resolution. Statements that start with, "You are…" or "You have…" often make the other party feel as though they are being attacked, and they may try to justify themselves in response. These statements often create defensive behavior that inhibits cooperation and encourages competition.

If you feel provoked or insulted by the other party, change the subject and address the negotiation climate rather than the subject matter. If the other party tries to intimidate you by shouting or to make you pity them by crying, the best thing to do is not react at all. Instead, take a break, wait for a little while and resume at a new, uncontroversial or shared point in the discussion as if nothing had happened. If you feel yourself starting to get too emotionally involved, take a deep breath, count slowly to five and then reply. Another way to manage your anger is to think of something pleasant. One of the best visions to use for this purpose is a mental picture of a beautiful sunset above the white sands of a deserted beach.

4) "I" & "We"

Use the word "I" when you are stating your own convictions. On the other hand, if you are talking about performance, always use the word "we" ("We have …", "We are …", "We think …") because everyone knows that a whole team stands behind a complex project.

On the other hand, when talking about defeats, use "I" ("I am disappointed that…", "I wonder why…"). It is less threatening for someone to hear your individual opinion than to be confronted with "we statements" that sound like accusations.

5) "Visualize" Your Arguments

Don't just make claims, but make your ideas clear with easy to follow steps. You can do this by using charts, graphs, or diagrams, or by using a flip chart or overheads. These visual aids make your arguments and your calculations easier to understand and accept.

6) All Is Well That Ends Well

At the end of the negotiations, summarize what was discussed. Repeat all of the important points that were agreed upon. Those points that are mentioned at the end usually stick best in peoples' minds, and both parties can walk away with the knowledge that they have reached a solution. When a group has been involved in the negotiations, it is wise to put these agreements on a flip chart for all to see and acknowledge. In the case of a personal discussion, a follow-up memo confirming the agreement is appropriate and minimizes the possibility of future misunderstandings.

≫ 9. 4 Skillful Questions in Negotiation

Skillfully formed questions show that you are listening attentively and that you are trying to figure out the motives and the background behind the others' argument. They also give you the opportunity to think things through and to elegantly change the direction of the discussion. Depending on the reply that you want to elicit out of the other party, you can work with different types of questions:

1) Open Questions

Open questions, such as, "What arguments are there against my suggestion?" encourage the other party to express their views and to tell you what they know about the issue. It makes the most sense to ask this type of question at the beginning of a dialogue in order to get into a topic and to uncover as much information as possible. Open questions almost always begin with "how", "what", and "why", and cannot be answered with a simple "yes" or "no".

2) Closed Questions

Closed questions are those that can be answered with "yes" or "no". They are most suitable for clarifying issues and concentrating the discussion on important points. However, if you ask several closed questions in a row, to which the answers are "yes", then the other party may feel intimidated and react aggressively.

3) Suggestive Questions

Suggestive questions are often lead-ins to assumptions or manipulations. Consider the question, "You want us to expand, don't you?" In such cases, the one asking the question is seldom interested in the other party's true opinion. The best way to handle such questions is not to reply or to reply with a counter question.

4) Indirect Questions

Indirect questions, otherwise known as trick questions, are often used in job interviews. For example, "How would your best friend describe you?" When it comes to these questions, you must be extremely careful with your reply, and anticipate such questions in advance.

When negotiating, use the question, "What would you suggest?" as often as possible. This will not only satisfy the other party, but will send the message that you are interested and listening. It also has the advantage of giving the other party the opportunity to express their opinion or make suggestions, which helps build a foundation of mutual respect.

≫ 9.5　Business Negotiation Etiquette in China

In China, while negotiating, only senior members of the negotiating team will speak. Foreign businessmen usually designate the most senior person in their group as their spokesman for the introductory functions.

Business negotiations occur at a slow pace. Foreign negotiators have to be prepared for the agenda to become a jumping off point for other discussions.

Chinese are non-confrontational. We will not overtly say "no", we will say "we will think about it" or "we will see". Chinese negotiations are process oriented. We want to determine if relationships can develop to a stage where both parties are comfortable doing business with the other. Decisions may take a long time, as we require careful review and consideration.

Under no circumstances should foreigner counterparts lose their temper or they will lose face and irrevocably damage their relationship.

Business is hierarchical. Decisions are unlikely to be made during the meetings. The Chinese are shrewd negotiators. The starting price should leave room for negotiation

Business attire is conservative and unpretentious. Men should wear dark colored, conservative business suits. Women should wear conservative business suits or dresses with a high neckline. Women should wear flat shoes or shoes with very low heels. Bright colors should be avoided.

Business cards are exchanged after the initial introduction. Foreign businessmen need to have one side of their business card translated into Chinese using simplified Chinese characters that are printed in gold ink since gold is an auspicious color. A business card should include one's title. If one's company is the oldest or largest in his country, that fact should be on his card as well.

Negotiators should hold the card in both hands when offering it, Chinese side facing the recipient.

≫ 9.6 Some Tips for Business Negotiators

Here are some pointers for business negotiators in their business negotiations:

1) Use Clever Phrases

To keep the negotiations from running headlong into a brick wall, do not always reply directly, but form your arguments wisely:

- Transform the argument: Instead of saying, "I see this differently..." you are better off saying, "You are talking about a problem that can be seen from many different angles. In this case, the most important thing is..."
- Reinterpret: Instead of saying, "I am of a completely different opinion..." say, "That is a good point, but I think we should also take...into consideration."
- Avoidance: Instead of saying, "No, that will never work..." say, "Yes, that is an important problem, but let's concentrate on the following situation for now..."
- Postponing an argument: Instead of saying, "We will not come to a solution that way..." you should say, "Before we come to a conclusion, we may want to consider..."

2) Dealing with Defeat

Be aware that negotiations are a constant game of give and take. Do not automatically consider a compromise as a defeat. Negotiations are not based on the principle of "all or nothing, win or lose". A negotiation strategy that focuses on destroying the other party or winning so they lose should not come into play because it does not focus on building fair and constructive business relationships. As Bismarck once said, "Whoever destroys his opponent, or wounds his opponent's pride, should be aware that he has created an enemy who will later seek revenge".

3) Impromptu Meetings

Even if you set up a meeting on short notice, make sure you inform others (the best way is via e-mail) as to what the meeting's focus and proposed agenda are. In this way, you give others time to prepare, and this will allow a more goal-oriented discussion.

≫ 9. 7　Skills and Strategies

1) Clarifying the stakes

(1) Can you speed up the process of checking inventory?

(2) We will only be able to give onsite management support services on a limited basis.

(3) The project blueprint you sent with the estimate is not quite what we had in mind.

(4) Do you think it would be possible to extend your confirmation deadline?

(5) The earlier I will be able to get back to you is tomorrow morning.

(6) If I made my guys stay over to check the inventory, I'll have to pay them at an overtime rate, which is time and a half.

2) Making concessions

(1) I really hope to reach an agreement with you today that is suitable and beneficial for us both.

(2) If you give us a discount of 7% on the high volume orders, we can pay in 60 days.

(3) A lower discount might be acceptable, if you handle the insurance fees.

(4) I can give you a better warranty if you would be willing to agree to an annual contract.

(5) I understand it's not the most convenient for you; perhaps we could shorten it to a sixth month contract if you are willing to take a lower rebate.

(6) Our delivery fee could be waived if you make an order of 50 units or more, but we would have to insist on the annual contract.

3) Discussing the bottom line

(1) We did the best that we could to give you a low price.

(2) I really want to work with you on this, but we've already gone as low as we can go.

(3) We're hoping to put together a really competitive bid, but we'd like to hit your target price too.

(4) Based on the estimated you gave us, by the time we figure in transportation and other expenses, our profit is shot.

(5) I've already given you a discount of 20% off of what we normally charge... if I go lower, we'll have loss on the project.

(6) We need an idea of your bottom line so that don't waste time with considerations that will overshoot your budget.

4) Accepting and confirming

(1) We agree to give you a break on the price, all together a discount of 6%.

(2) So, if all this is agreeable to you, I'll put it all down on paper and fax a contract to you this afternoon.

(3) We've agreed to final price of $ 1,500 per container, to be paid by wire transfer within a 60 day period.

(4) If you can get a signed version of the contract we've agreed upon back to me by tomorrow morning, we can go head and make arrangements to ship the product on Monday.

(5) If there's nothing else to discuss, then I'll have my secretary draw up a contract and get it to you before the end of the day.

(6) So far, we've confirmed our price and payment arrangements, now let's get down to the transportation and insurance fees...

| Chapter 10 | # Business Etiquette in Travel |

In a business world, travel may be a part of businessmen's daily routine, they may commute to work every day, or they may travel around the globe to visit their other offices. Whatever the case may be, there are some travel etiquette that every person should know before traveling.

≫ 10.1 Travel Etiquettes

As a representative of your company, whether this will be your first or your thousandth business trip, you should be conscious of conduct that is considered proper during your absence from the office. You need to know how to behave appropriately on a business trip.

First, you need to pack all essential items in a carry-on bag to avoid being ill-prepared for business if the airline loses your luggage. Showing up for a trade show or a meeting with a client dressed in yesterday's clothes will not make a positive impression.

Second, you should dress professionally during the entire trip. Your attire should reflect the fact that you are on a business trip, whether you are on a plane, on a golf course or in a conference room.

Third, you will have to be prepared and be on time. You may normally arrive at the office at 8:10 every morning and not speak until after your first cup of coffee, but clients will not take kindly to your decision to be 10 minutes late for an important meeting and still needing to go over your notes.

Forth, you are required to use proper business language. Even though some business trips may include more casual situations, such as lunch, dinner or even golf, keep in mind that you are still representing your company, and like the old saying goes, "Loose lips sink ships".

Fifth, you should brush up on table manners and the basics of business etiquette before you go. This may help you avoid an embarrassing gaffe while on your trip.

Last but not the least, you must save all receipts from your trip so you can easily determine your expenses when you return and conduct yourself with grace and decorum at all times. If you are uncertain about these terms, consider buying a book on business etiquette for some light reading while on the plane.

≫ 10. 2   The Basic Rules for a Business Trip

When we plan a business trip, it is not just a matter of booking accommodation and offsite airport parking. We also need to think about what we are going to do when we get to our destination. Every country has different customs, so what works well in one might be totally out of the question in another. To do business, we will need to think about the basic rules. Here they are:

1) Appearance

This is one of the most important. Appearance includes items such as our clothing, body language and gestures. For example, it's important to know whether our new business colleagues will expect us to dress conservatively, formally or at the height of fashion. If we are in Italy, for example, wearing unfashionable clothes may affect the way we are perceived. Western women doing business in the United Arab Emirates may need to dress more modestly than if they were at home. Watch out for gestures — it is easy to cause offence if we use the wrong ones.

2) Behavior

Behavior covers a wide range of areas, including how meetings are run, protocol, negotiating with others, dining and giving gifts. For example, personal space requirements vary from place to place — and even within the same country. One analysis of the behavior of English and French speaking Canadians suggest that Francophone Canadians require less personal space. Punctuality is another issue — if we book a meeting in England, know that people will expect us to turn up on time, or even a little early. In the UAE, crossing our legs to show the soles of our feet is considered offensive.

3) Communication

Even casual conversation holds pitfalls for the unwary. In the UK, someone who has been knighted is referred to by title and first name in conversation, for example, Sir James. In the UAE, don't discuss women. In some countries, such as Japan, speakers prefer not to use the word "no", which means that sometimes *yes* may actually mean *no* — and it's not the only place where that happens. In India, it's considered more polite to say "I'll try" than to give an outright refusal.

≫ **10. 3　Planning a Business Trip**

When you plan a business trip, you can search for the best route online, and make travel arrangements that are both cost effective and comfortable. And it's not just the actual flight you can book — you can also pre-book accommodation, offsite airport parking, rental cars and sightseeing trips.

Fly direct if you can, but if you can't, then leave some flexibility in the schedule. This is good both for missed connections and for your own health. Making your connection a couple hours later than your inward flight will free you from a possible five mile jog across an airport with your luggage.

You need choose a reliable airline. Many sites offer data on which airlines experience fewest delays. This could make your journey much more pleasant. If you are a frequent flyer, then pick an airline that serves most of your regular destinations and join the frequent flyer program. That will give you lots of travel perks, and it works for airlines, car hire and parking too.

If you're on a short trip, travel light with just a laptop and a carry-on. This will cut down on security checks and make it quicker to leave the airport at your destination. If you are on a longer trip, keep important documents with you (you can print them out ahead of time) so you won't have to worry about messing up an important presentation if your luggage goes missing or gets damaged. You can also use travel time to study any important notes or documents before your meeting.

Technology is your friend. With a good cell phone, pager, laptop or any combination of the three, you don't need to leave the rest of your work behind when you're on a business trip. You can keep tabs on the latest information and handle urgent situations while heading to your next destination.

You should allow for some down time. If you're lucky, your company is flexible about the fact that you're traveling on your own time. Leave some time to relax and have fun. It will help you be a more effective business person and will protect your health too.

Finally, if you are a regular traveler, make a checklist for everything you need to accomplish before you travel and print it out before your next trip. This will streamline your travel arrangements and remove even more of the stress from your business trip.

≫ **10. 4　Business Travel Protocols and Etiquette**

The world has changed dramatically and now it is no longer a nicety to have international etiquette training but a necessity to succeed.

To survive, we must be able to compete in a truly global economy, and to compete effectively we must understand more about other countries, other cultures, other ways of doing business. To illustrate this point, examine this example, a member of the U. S. Congress traveled to Moscow in the winter of 1992—the worst winter many Russians had experienced since World War II. Food was scarce and people had to wait in long lines everywhere. Much to the horror of his escorts, he complained because he couldn't get his bacon and eggs for breakfast.

It's really a matter of putting yourself in your European colleague's place. In this example, you are the host and you are having European guest, you expect your European guest to have at least a rudimentary knowledge of your country and customs. The more knowledge your guest has, the more favorably impressed you will be. Europeans feel the same way about you when you are a guest in their country. If you are ignorant of their country and culture, you create the impression that you're boorish or, worse, that you don't care enough about them to spend a little time learning about their country and culture. That's not the kind of impression that leads to a good business relationship. A point to remember is that in Europe and most other countries, business is done based on relationships

Cultural differences and language barriers are common excuses for insensitive behavior. To create favorable relationships requires a willingness to listen, understand and accept the differences. Approach going abroad as if you were invited to your boss' home for a party, assuming you would like a raise or promotion. If you enter a host country with this attitude, you'll be sensitive, well-dressed, bring an appropriate gift and take the time to learn the customs and behaviors that will make you a gracious guest and leave them with a favorable first impression.

Doing your homework before you visit any country is essential, once there here are some general pointers:

- When visiting a country, know the name of their president or prime minister, their political system, language spoken, official name of the country and the collective name of its people.
- Most Europeans shake hands with everyone present when arriving and again when leaving.
- Be prepared to receive and to give a lighter less firm handshake in many countries.
- Always remove your gloves before shaking hands (something President Bush forgot to do this past year and it was noticed worldwide).
- Never shake hands with one hand in your pocket.
- In Europe, don't use first names until you are explicitly invited to do so by your host. We consider using first names as friendly but Europeans definitely don't. Using first names that quickly makes them feel uncomfortable.
- Attempt to speak the language of your host country, even if you can only manage a few polite phrases.
- Never use slang terms, idioms, sports analogies or colloquialisms, for example: "I was tickled to death. We've got you covered. I got a kick out of it."
- Never slap people on the back.

● Gift-giving customs vary from country to country, make sure to observe them. Keep this in mind: Never be tacky, violate tradition, or send intimate items.

≫ 10.5 Travel Etiquette in the World's Most-Visited Countries

1) France

Dining:

Never eat fruit whole. Peel and slice it.

Don't cut your crusty baguette — break it with your fingers.

Don't order a Martini or Scotch before dinner; they're considered palate numbing.

General:

The French value their privacy — don't be nosy.

Avoid using any of the following in public: nail clippers, combs, toothpicks, chewing gum. And while you're at it, don't scratch or yawn either.

The French don't make or tell jokes.

2) The Unites States

Dining:

Never arrive early to a dinner party.

If you are offered a second helping of food, feel free to take as much as you want. Americans like people to eat well.

General:

"See you later," is just a farewell expression; it doesn't mean anything. Same with "How are you?" ("Fine!" "Great!" Doing well are only appropriate responses.)

Smile. Americans like to smile and be smiled at.

Try to avoid silence; it makes Americans uncomfortable.

3) U. K.

Dining:

You should leave a very small amount of food on your plate when finished eating.

Leave a dinner party shortly after dinner ends.

Wait for your host to begin eating before digging in.

General:

Handshakes are light, not firm.

Do not push, shove or cut in line.

Always hold the door for the person behind you.

4) Italy

Dining:

Don't roll pasta on your spoon — do it on the sides of your plate.

Burping is considered extremely vulgar.

Keep both hands above the table while you're eating, but keep the elbows off.

General:

Italians are *chic*. Dress elegantly but conservatively.

Try not to yawn or remove your shoes in public.

Italians are generous; they'll forgive most faux pas except arrogance and rudeness.

5) Spain

Dining:

No bread and butter plate is used; bread is set directly on the table.

Spaniards don't waste food. Don't take what you don't think you can eat.

General:

Be patient; expect to be interrupted when talking.

It is acceptable and common to be 30 minutes late to social functions in Southern Spain, 15 minutes in Northern Spain. Never be late for a bullfight.

Tip everyone for everything.

6) China

Dining:

Feel free to *belch* and *slurp* soup while eating.

Eating rare beef is considered barbaric.

Leave some food on your plate to honor the generosity of the host.

Be ready to make a small toast for any and all occasions.

General:

If a Chinese person greets you with applause, applaud back.

Clicking fingers and whistling is considered very rude.

Show special respect for older people — offer chairs, etc.

Never point with your index finger.

7) Austria

Dining:

Never cut a dumpling with a knife; break it apart with your fork.

Don't discuss business during a meal unless the host brings it up.

The person who extends the invitation to a restaurant will generally pay the bill — don't hassle over it.

General

Avoid wearing shorts while shopping.

Shake hands with everyone — men, women and children — before a social or business meeting.

Austrians insist on punctuality for social engagements.

8) Germany

Dining:

Use a fork and knife to eat sandwiches, fruit and most other food.

"Guten appetit" is said before eating and means "enjoy your meal". It is the host's way of saying, "Please start".

General:

Introduce yourself by your last name only — never use your title.

Stand when an elder or high-ranked person enters the room.

Compliment sparingly — it may embarrass people.

Germans are more formal and punctual than the rest of the world. Try to follow suit.

9) Russia

Dining:

Drinking tends to be an all-or-nothing affair. Know your limits.

If invited to a meal, don't make post-dinner plans. You're expected to stick around and socialize.

General:

Learning Russian is the best way to win friends and influence people. At least try.

Expect demonstrative greetings — hugs, backslaps, etc.

Don't shake hands over a threshold. Russians believe this will lead to an argument.

10) Mexico

Dining:

Don't leave the table immediately after you finish eating.

Drinking to excess is frowned upon in Mexico, especially when done by women.

Always keep both hands above the table.

General:

Get accustomed to people standing close to you.

It's OK to be late to a social engagement. In fact, you should be late, or you'll wait for hours for others to arrive.

≫ 10.6 Some Tips for Business Trip

1) The World's Best and Worst Airport

Are you planning a trip? Then these lists might be useful. CNN has a list of the world's best airports which have consistently been top rated over several years. These are:
- Hong Kong International Airport
- Changi International Airport, Singapore
- Incheon International Airport, Seoul, South Korea
- Kuala Lumpur International Airport, Malaysia
- Munich Airport, Germany

The news site also has a feature on the world's worst airports:
- Baghdad International Airport, Iraq
- Indira Gandhi International Airport, Delhi, India
- Lukla Airport, Nepal
- Leopold Sedar Senghor International Airport, Senegal
- Los Angeles International Airport, USA
- London Heathrow, UK
- Charles de Gaulle International Airport, Paris, France

2) How to Make a Hotel Room Feel like Home

- Choose a hotel that's in close proximity to your meeting or client. Ask your client if they have a company discount with the hotel.
- Use the promise of a long stay (or if you will return often over a period of time), as leverage to ask for extras.
- Look for hotels with in-room amenities: voice mail availability, two-line speaker phone, fax/printer/copier, ergonomic chair, 24-hour room service, coffeemaker and ironing board.

3) Tips & Warnings for Business Trip

- Ask if you can smoke before lighting up. Smoking has become something of a social and business faux pas in recent years, and if your companion or client is not smoking, asking permission is essential.
- Use a personal phone card to make long-distance phone calls while you are away. This way, you won't have to reimburse the company for these charges on the hotel bill.
- Traveling in foreign countries can be tricky. Before you leave, make sure to buy a guidebook or consult someone who has recently traveled to your intended destination to learn about the

culture and customs.

- Avoid planning leisure-time activities during your trip if they will detract from the amount of business you are able to conduct. If you stay out until 2 a. m. or get a sunburn at the pool, you won't be at the top of your game for business the next day.

- Stay away from pornography, alcohol and anything potentially inappropriate during your trip. This includes renting adult films in your hotel room, visiting bars and being in any situation that could result in your being arrested and, ultimately, fired.

- Keep in mind that your time is not your own on a business trip. You belong to your employer during this time; you're not being paid to goof off.

≫ 10. 7 Skills and Strategies

1) By taxi

(1) Bring / Drive me to the Beijing Hotel, please.

(2) Could you carry this luggage in the trunk?

(3) CanI get back to my hotel quickly from here by taxi?

(4) Do you know where this address is?

(5) I will pay as much as it says on the meter.

(6) I am late, please hurry up.

2) By subway

(1) Excuse me, can you help me to figure out how to get to the Hongshan subway station from here.

(2) You get a daily pass that will allow you to travel unlimited for the whole day for about 10 yuan.

(3) Zhongshan is a big station, so there will likely be a lot of people getting off at that stop.

(4) You can transfer to the lightrail at that station, you'll have to exit the subway and present the unused portion of your combination ticket to the taskmaster.

(5) How frequent is this subway service?

3) By air

(1) I'd like to take the flight tomorrow afternoon and come back next Saturday afternoon.

(2) I'd like a round-trip ticket to New York, please.

(3) I'd like a one-way ticket to Paris.

(4) Could you direct me to gate 18, please?

(5) What is the actual flying time from here to Paris?

(6) What is the local time when we land in Los Angeles?

4) At hotel

(1) I am wondering if you have any vacancies tomorrow? I'd like book a double room with a bath.

(2) CanI reserve a single room on the night of May twenty-second?

(3) What is the rate for a room per night? Are meals included?

(4) I would like to check in, please. My name is Wang Ming.

(5) Will you tell me how to telephone outside the hotel?

(6) I would like to check out. Please make up my bill.

Chapter 11

Business Etiquette
in Socializing

Good social manners play an important and integral role in every family or friendly relationship. We also use some of our polished social manners in each business venture in everyday business life. Whether you are at a business meal or event, networking with clients, a job interview or even a sales call, etiquette is an important factor in business.

≫ 11. 1　Socializing Etiquette

It is equally important in every social situation you find yourself. Your comfort level increases dramatically when you feel comfortable with what to do and say in any situation. You attain confidence and show authority when you are not wondering if you are acting properly.

Having well-rounded socializing skills are not an option, but a necessity of business life. Most people looking to move up the corporate ladder realize the importance of mastering job-related skills. But what they may not also know is that soft skills — the way they carry themselves, dress, interact with others — can be just as important in determining whether they will or will not be promoted, and may even be creating a negative image without their knowledge. For example, if there were two managers who were competing for the same promotion. Both were equally technically competent and mentally ready for the move. Yet, one had outstanding social skills, dressed for the position and could easily strike up a conversation with anyone. The other was sloppy in appearance, hid in a corner and had poor eye contact at social events. Guess who got the promotion?

Conversely, there are also many professionals who think that they are great at networking, making small talk, and connecting with people when in reality they exude an unprofessional image. With this in mind, here are a few tips on how to improve:

1) Set Goals

Where do you want to be in one, three and five years from now? Do you want a promotion? A new job or career? What are you willing to do to achieve them? Write them down and review them periodically to keep on track.

2) Take a Good Look at Yourself or Better Yet, Ask Your Mentor for Feedback

Unfortunately, we never see ourselves as others do. If you are not getting the results you want, ask for feedback from others to better understand what is holding you back.

3) Commit to the Change You Want to Create

To make any change in behavior you must practice the new skill repeatedly for twenty-one days. Set aside time to do this and make it a priority.

4) Dress Appropriately

Wear clothes that fit well and are appropriate for each business occasion. Understand the difference between traditional business attire and the different levels of business casual. Wear clothes that say you are there for business and should be taken seriously. If you wear it to the beach, on a hot date, or to the park — it's not appropriate for business. With that in mind, keep mini-skirts, T-shirts with slogans, overalls, low-cut tops, sandals, jean jackets, sneakers and zip-front hooded sweatshirts for your weekend or at-home wardrobe only.

5) Learn How to Properly Shake Hands

Touch thumb joint to thumb joint. Make it firm — not a bone crusher or a loose fish handshake. People form an impression of you by your greeting. Make sure they've formed a good one.

6) Keep Your Body Language Open

In business, many professionals are not aware of how they are communicating with their body. Fidgeting or not making eye contact, will give you away. Keep a smile on your face and your body language open.

7) Fake It Until You Feel It

If you feel as if you have already achieved your goal, it will happen. Individuals that maintain an upbeat attitude portray a positive image and attract positive company.

8) Remember "Successful People Look Successful!"

By remembering these points, you can help to more quickly advance your career.

≫ 11. 2　Ways of Addressing People

How to address your boss and colleagues? That is the question. It is a headache for some 40 percent of people starting out on their careers according to the latest survey conducted by recruitment website Zhaopin. com of 6,000 working people, as cited by today's *Oriental Morning Post*.

In the results Zhaopin disclosed, 23 percent of novice employees are at a loss as to how to address their bosses and colleagues, while one-third said they have quickly managed to get accustomed to their companies' style of address. Only 5 percent saw it as no problem at all.

The survey indicates most working people prefer to be addressed directly by their Chinese names (66 percent), or, less favored, by their English names (17 percent). Fewer — still like to be addressed by their titles (7 percent) or as sisters or brothers (5 percent).

In reality, on business occasions, most people address their customers by their titles (65 percent) such as "manager", and many like to use Ms. or Mr. (31 percent). Only 3 percent use the other parties' English names and 1 percent adopt "comrade", the previously popular form of address.

English names are most often used in foreign companies (31 percent) while titles are most favored in state-owned enterprises (45 percent).

When addressing bosses, using titles scored highest, at 33 percent, among all types of enterprise and nicknames were the least used (2 percent). Chinese names (16 percent), English names (9 percent) and addressing someone as "teacher" (8 percent) were also used.

≫ 11. 3　Some Guidelines to Socialize Successfully

Employees welcome chances to get to know the boss as a person, not just a manager. During the frenetic work week, they encounter the boss as the source of discipline, assignments, occasional reprimands and, typically, very little personal chit chat. So it's refreshing to be around the supervisor when she showcases her humor, asks about your family and hobbies, and gives an unrestrained laugh. However, both employees and bosses should be aware that the social scene does not erase the workplace lines of authority.

If your boss likes your personality at a party, that does not mean you will get the next promotion, which depends instead on your professional skills. Here are seven guidelines that every employer and employee should keep in mind for after-hours mingling:

1) Avoid off Color Humor

The jokes you would tell your golf buddies could jeopardize your professional reputation if you share them with workplace colleagues, no matter how informal the setting is. True, they might laugh out of courtesy, or may be from discomfort. Yet you risk losing their respect. Play safe. Don't tell any joke that you wouldn't tell at an office staff meeting.

2) Refrain from Touching

Refrain from touching other than a handshake greeting, unless you happen to go dancing with the group. Draping an arm around a colleague might prompt an eventual lawsuit, especially when you don't give that person an expected raise. And the employee who caresses the boss can create an image of fakery and pandering.

3) Drink Moderately

Every year, holiday parties, company picnics and similar outings become career graveyards for bosses and employees who want to become "the life of the party". Sometimes we assume that two more drinks will help us talk more easily. That's a mistake. Two more drinks will encourage you to talk more — period. The impaired speaking and unsteady walk that follow those extra cocktails could brand you: "lush," "a drunk," "undisciplined," or something similar.

Along those lines, never mention that drinking is important to you. Stay away from "Nothing like a stiff drink at the end of the day to help a guy unwind". Whimsically, we slip into comments like that, such as "Thought that bartender would never bring our order". Although you are trying to inject a bit of levity into the conversation, the quips could backfire, categorizing you as a problem drinker.

4) Make Sure You Circulate

Make sure you circulate among everyone present, not just the managerial group you feel most comfortable with. The person who talks with his or her clique and avoids everyone else nullifies the inclusive good will the event is intended to foster. Spend time with line employees as well as "the suits".

5) Avoid Shop Talk

Demonstrate that you have an interesting, meaningful life away from the corporation. Nobody wants to hear your opinions about a five year plan, a drop in sales or the employee you had to fire. As an old song advises, "talk happy talk, things that people like to hear". Stay well informed about major sporting events, releases of new movies, great places to vacation, new restaurants your friends have recommended, bestselling books and national events. Definitely, party goers want to talk about them, not corporate problems and plans.

6) Listen Attentively

Good listeners become our favorite people. We move away from motor-mouths who dominate conversations. Encourage others to talk, with comments like "very interesting," "tell me more," and "What happened next?"

Seek first to understand, and then to be understood. " Follow that advice, and you'll become the hit of the company's social outing".

7) Mind Your Manners

If the occasion includes a meal, pay special attention to your table etiquette. You want to look like you belong at top-tier banquets. Illustrate that you have acquired polish and grace.

≫ 11. 4   Online Socializing Etiquette

If you're new to the online socializing scene, there are a few common mistakes you may want to try to avoid making as you venture forth. Even if you're just interested in making new friends or finding travel companions, these simple tips will help you make a better first impression online.

1) Taking too Long to Respond to Messages

It's just like your Mom used to say, "Promptness is a virtue". In fact, responding to an e-mail in a timely fashion not only shows you're interested (or not), it also shows you have good manners — which are still something most people value.

2) Getting too Personal too Soon

Don't ask for too much personal info right up front. Take your time. Would you feel good about telling someone the intimate details of your life, right off the bat?

3) Not Logging in Often Enough

If you don't log in frequently, you'll not only miss messages. You may also send out "signals" that you're just not that interested in meeting people.

4) Sending One Word Replies Only

Come on! You've got a good imagination. Send a message that says a little something about you, your interests, and your dreams.

5) Making Overt Sexual Overtures Right Away

It doesn't matter how hot or sexy you think someone is. Being too upfront about your desires too quickly could end up driving (or scaring) them away.

6) Staying with the First Online Site You Join

Different online communities offer different things. Some put the onus on sex only. Others are for specific interest and/or ethnic groups. Some cater to everyone from the age of 18 to 80+. Try to find one that fits your life, lifestyle and interests.

7) Posting a Bad Photo of Yourself, or Not Posting One at All

Not everyone is photogenic, but take some time to find a good shot of yourself — preferably showing you smiling and looking directly into the camera. Shy? Don't be — profiles with photos get looked at 10 times more than those without.

8) Writing Boring Subject Lines

When you write an e-mail message try to picture yourself on the receiving end and ask yourself, "Would I open this message?" The more intriguing the subject line, the higher the chances are that it will get opened.

9) Being too Vague

Everyone likes to feel special. So when you find someone you're interested in contacting, take a moment to read his or her profile carefully. Then, when you send them a message, include some of the interests/activities/life experiences you have in common.

10) Exaggerating or Lying About Yourself

It may seem like a good idea at first, but what are you going to do if you eventually meet someone in person?

11) Spending too Little Time on Your Life Experience Profile

Sure, entering your profile takes time. But you're an interesting person who's had an interesting life. Make sure your profile reflects who you really are or you'll end up short-changing yourself in the long run.

12) Bad Spelling

Nothing says laziness and/or ignorance like a profile or e-mail message that's littered with spelling errors. Take your time, use Spell Check if you have it, and type carefully.

≫ **11. 5   Office Collections and Parties**

Many offices are virtual beehives of social life, complete with their own patterns of gift-giving, party schedules, and customs and traditions.

1) Collections

It is the custom in many American offices to take up collections to buy presents for births, weddings, birthdays, and other happy occasions. Many people willingly participate in this tradition, but many more undoubtedly resent the continual expense.

Office collections only work among coworkers who genuinely have some fondness for one another and when the demands aren't too high. They don't work when you're in an enormous office and you barely recognize the person to whom you're expected to give money. They also don't work when a set amount, which is often beyond some people's means, is expected.

Asking people to kick in a dollar or two is okay. Asking for ten or twenty dollars usually is not. Those who know the person and want to give more money may, but no one should ever feel obliged to give more than a dollar or two to an office collection.

If you're taking up the collection, you can ease the situation by asking only those who really know the recipient to participate. Rather than exclude anyone, though, offer the choice to someone who may not want to contribute: "I'm taking up a collection to buy Mary a wedding gift, but I know you don't know her, so I don't feel it's right to ask you. " That leaves the decision entirely in the hands of the giver. From the giver's point of view, once someone has let you off the hook in this way, you should feel no pressure to contribute. Another solution used in some offices is to pass around an envelope. Each person may anonymously contribute what he or she likes.

2) Office Parties

Another office tradition is giving parties to celebrate big events — baby showers, wedding showers, retirement parties, and the ubiquitous birthday parties. Strictly speaking, these ought not to be held on office time or premises, but they often are. Whenever possible, give major parties for coworkers at another location. Parties that take place at work, say, for a retirement or a birthday, should be kept fairly brief and subdued. Some large offices merge events — that is, they have one birthday party in a month rather than a series of birthday celebrations.

3) Gifts-giving

Most offices indulge in some form of gift-giving, usually at holiday time. Bosses typically give gifts to their staff members, while employees are not obliged to give gifts in return. The exception is the secretary or personal assistant who wishes to give the boss a present. This gift can be very modest, even if the boss's gift was lavish. It would, in fact, be inappropriate for an employee to give an employer an elaborate or expensive gift. Some offices have a grab bag gift exchange, where everyone puts his name in a bag also draws the name of another worker. When these are the custom, the gifts should be small, and it is a good idea to set a dollar limit, usually five to ten dollars.

The best office gifts are impersonal but clearly chosen with an individual's interests in mind. Books, compact discs, food, desk accessories, date-books, umbrellas, and impersonal items of clothing such as scarves and gloves are all acceptable. Joke gifts are fine and popular in many offices as long as they are not overly offensive.

Employers should also keep in mind that a bonus is not a present. It is part of the reimbursement package and as such should never be referred to or considered a present. Apart from any specific office rituals, gift exchanges among coworkers are the same as gift exchanges among friends.

≫ 11. 6   Some Tips for Socializing

1) Effective Ways to Improve One's Social Skills

We may find some people are very shy and have difficulty in interacting with others. Some people who were previously outgoing may encounter problems in life, which result in a shy demeanor. To be shy can be a stumbling block in situations where social interaction is important, such as giving a speech, working on a project with a group. The following are the effective ways to overcoming a shy demeanor:

a. Attend Social Functions as Often as You Can

No matter it is a holiday party for your company, a birthday bash with your friends, or a business reception, you can use these situations to practice your skills. Talk to the people you know to warm up to the group and then expand out and talk to new people. Over time, talking to others becomes easier.

b. Find a Hobby or Organization That Gets You out of the House and Around Other People Who Share Your Interests

In general, people may find it much easier to talk to one with whom they share interests because they do not need to struggle to find something to talk about. Thus, finding a hobby or organization that gets you out of the house and around other people who share your interests, you will find it easier to talk to them.

c. Branch out from Your Usual Group of Friends

While it is easier to have someone you know to talk to initially, it is always easier to socialize with people you already know. Meeting new people is a big stumbling block for a shy person. Join one of your friends at an event you normally would not attend to expand the number of people you are exposed to.

d. Watch How Other People Interact with Each Other

Watching how other people interact with each other to learn what is expected in social situations. If you aren't comfortable jumping into a social situation right away, you can still benefit by observing those around you. Once you have a feel for what is going on around you, it may be easier to jump in.

e. Give Yourself Time to Get Used to Social Situations

You must recognize if a situation is too uncomfortable to even attempt or if you need to push yourself to join in. You can always give it a try and if you still feel uncomfortable, wait and try again later on.

f. Change Your Attitude About Yourself

If you constantly tell yourself that you are shy so you can't do it, you will believe that. Instead, tell yourself repeatedly that you are confident and brave and you can talk to others and socialize. Forget about what other people may think of you. Keep your attitude positive and your behavior will follow.

g. Volunteer with on Organization

Volunteering with an organization, such as a food kitchen, senior center or youth organization, where you can help serve others and enhance your social skills. Helping others can help take your mind off the social aspects and allow you to interact with others naturally without having to think about it.

2) The Effective Way to Creating a Social Group

Setting up a social group is a very effective way to meet business counterparts in your area who have the same interests with you and you can meet to discuss similar interests and socialize with each other. Creating a social group is not very difficult task, but it takes time. Bear the following instructions in mind if you want creating a successful social group:

a. Develop a Central Theme for Your Social Organization

This should be based on your interests and can be virtually any theme. For instance, if you are very concerned with women's rights, make this the focus of your organization.

b. Write down a List of Criteria People Must Meet in Order to Join

Though many groups are open groups, you should lay out some guidelines. For example, you might indicate that members must be of a certain age or if the group is for women only.

c. Create Fliers and Distribute Them Around Your Area

Try to post the fliers in areas where they will be seen by people with a similar interest. Make sure the fliers have your contact information so potential members have a means of contacting you.

d. Make a Face Book Group

Twitter account or blog for your social organization. Having an online presence will help you reach out to more people with similar interests.

e. Book a Meeting Location and Set up a Meet and Greet for the New Members of Your Group

Booking a meeting location and set up a meet and greet for the new members of your group. Once enough people have contacted you expressing their interest in the group, set up a time to meet and, from there, you can book regular meetings.

⋙　**11. 7　Skills and Strategies**

1) Finding out the topic

(1) How's the weather tomorrow?

(2) What's it like outside? Hot?

(3) A love day, isn't it?

(4) What do you like? Sports?

(5) How long does it take you to commute?

(6) What are your hobbies?

2) Small talks

(1) Is this the first conference you've been to?

(2) Where do you want to go next year?

(3) How long have you been in your present position?

(4) How do you get along with your coworkers?

(5) You haven't changed a bit, very young and beautiful!

(6) Your daughter is really out of this world!

3) Signaling the end of a conversation

(1) It's been interesting talking to you.

(2) I enjoyed meeting you.

(3) Hope to see you again someday.

(4) We have to make plans to get together sometime.

(5) Come and see me when you are free.

(6) Let's go to dinner sometime.

4) Ending a telephone conversation

(1) There is someone on the other line. Can we continue this later?

(2) Someone is at the door. I'll call you back later.

(3) Sorry, my other line is ringing. Bye.

(4) I have to get back to work. I must say good-bye now.

(5) Something has come up. I'll call again later.

(6) OK, don't forget to give me a call.

5) Farewells

(1) We'd like to thank you for coming, and we hope you enjoyed your time with us today.

(2) We'll be sure to keep in touch.

(3) Can I call you a taxi to take you back?

(4) If you're ever in London, be sure to look me up.

(5) Even though this was a rushed trip, I really had a very good time and I look forward to the next opportunity we have to visit again.

(6) I am glad you had a chance to visit our headquarters, and I hope you can come back soon.

Chapter 12

Business Etiquette
in Gift-giving

When doing business in different countries and cultures it can be difficult to know what to give as a gift. Gift-giving has in fact grown in importance due to the increase in international trade and has become an extension of the business relationship. Both sides now see gift-giving as both a way of firming up a relationship as well as representing their culture in the best light.

≫ 12. 1　Some Basic Rules on Business Gift-giving

Gift-giving can be a minefield if thought about too much. In principle there are a few simple guidelines people should stick to when giving gifts and the rest is up to common sense. The following tips will help chose the gift that will be appropriate, appreciated, and remembered.

1) Being Culturally Aware

When giving a gift in a foreign country, do your homework to find out if there are any dos and don'ts when it comes to exchanging gifts. Ten minutes research can save a lot of embarrassment. Pay attention to areas such as what gifts are culturally inappropriate, what to wrap them in and how to give/accept them.

2) Use Personal Interests

Do some digging on your client/customer and try to find gifts that fit with their interests. Do they support a certain sports teams or like a specific game? Do they have a favorite band or like a certain food? Picking up on their interests will show your attention to detail and result in a better relationship. Do some digging on your client/customer and try to find gifts that fit with their interests. Do they support a certain sports teams or like a specific game? Do they have a favorite band or like a certain food? Picking up on their interests will show your attention to detail and result in a better relationship.

3) Obey Company Rules

Always find out if there are any formal rules with regards to gift-giving in a company. Some have strict policies on what can or cannot be accepted. For example, many companies now place restrictions on the value of a gift that can be accepted. If you don't like the idea of asking your client, then ask their PA or receptionist instead.

4) Use the Logo

Whether or not to use the logo is a difficult question. Some people may find it a bit of marketing ploy and not take kindly to it. Others may see it as a nice touch. The best advice is that if you must give a gift with your logo on it, keep it small and subtle.

When it comes to gift-giving etiquette the best advice is to use your common sense and seek out the experiences of others. Gifts vary in importance from culture to culture so make sure that the gift you give is deemed proper for that particular country, person or company.

≫ 12. 2   Selecting a Corporate Gift

Selecting a gift for someone that you do business with, whether it is a boss, coworker, or client can be tricky business over the holidays. When choosing a corporate gift this year there are many things to keep in mind to help you make sure you're using proper gift-giving etiquette.

One of the first things that you should do before you choose a gift is to **check the corporate policy**. Many companies have a "no-gift" policy and giving a gift under these circumstances may result in trouble for the recipient. Even a gift-given with the best intentions can be a problem if that gift violates the corporate policy. The best way to find out if gift-giving is allowed is to contact the Personnel Department of the company in question for their guidelines. They will be able to tell you if your gift is allowed and appropriate.

Gift-giving should be done only when you are currently doing business with the organization that you want to gift. Make sure that you do not give gifts to organizations that you are negotiating with. These well-meaning gifts may be misconstrued as a bribe and it would be inappropriate to give a gift in this situation.

Great people to give gifts to this season are **long-term clients**. These are the clients who pay their bills, and have stuck with you over a period of time. Examples of these people would be sub-contractors that you regularly work with, your postal carrier, your accountant, or lawyer, as well as any other professionals that you rely on to run your business in the day to day. These are the people who often go un-thanked and therefore, the holidays are an excellent time to remember those who help you conduct your business.

If you are looking to give a gift to several people within a company and want to forgo individual gift-giving, as it may seem too personal, consider sending a gift that can be **shared**. These types of gifts include gourmet food baskets, or other types of gifts that include non-perishable goodies. Be sure to avoid items that require preparation, are perishable, or contain alcohol.

A great tip for corporate gift-giving is to **tailor the gift to the person** who will be receiving it. If you are giving a gift to an individual, try to find something that reflects the person's hobbies or interests, if they are known. Be sure to not get something that would be too personal or embarrassing, especially if you are giving a gift to someone of the opposite gender.

Whenever possible, try to **deliver your gift personally**. If this is not possible, include a brief, personalized, hand-written note. This will add an additional element of generosity as well as let your recipient know how much you care. In a world where everything is shipped, it is nice to receive a gift that is hand delivered.

If you choose to add your logo to a gift, be sure to keep it small and discreet so that the gift doesn't appear to be an advertisement. Also, never put a logo on an item that you intend to be a personal gift.

Items that are commonly given, but rarely appreciated are "necessity" items such as mouse pads and mugs. Giving these items may make you look insensitive and are extremely impersonal. Instead consider a calendar with motivational sayings, or a beautifully potted plant, if you are looking for something for their office. Try to add a personal touch to show you care to any item you give.

Setting a budget is very important when purchasing business gifts. Spending too little or too much can create uncomfortable situations where the recipient either feels you are being cheap, or is uncomfortable with your extravagance. Make sure you know your recipient and choose the appropriate gift.

Make sure your holiday gift-giving goes smoothly this year when selecting your business gifts. Keep in mind these guidelines and you are sure to choose a gift your recipient will truly appreciate. Make sure your holiday gift-giving goes smoothly this year when selecting your business gifts. Keep in mind these guidelines and you are sure to choose a gift your recipient will truly appreciate.

≫ 12. 3 Business Gift-giving Etiquette

In general gifts are given in business to promote goodwill and foster good relationships. They are also given to show appreciation. How do you know what is a proper gift?

First, if you are dealing in international trade you should make yourself knowledgeable about the customs of those you would like to gift. For example, if you are dealing with oil barons or emirates from the Middle East you wouldn't want to give them a gift of wood no matter how intricate. The reason is that they perceive would to be of very low value, not making any brownie points there.

Another big consideration is to give a gift that you know the recipient will appreciate. Do a little research; find out what their interests and hobbies are. They will be very impressed that you took the time to discover what they like and will feel comfortable in knowing that this wasn't just some anonymous purchase.

Gag gifts are almost always inappropriate, especially if there is a sexual connotation. Lingerie should never be given as a business gift. This is an intimate gift reserved for those in a close personal relationship.

Other gifts to be careful of giving are food and alcohol which are very popular during the holidays. Prime examples would be giving a gift of lobster or a gift basket with pork sausage to a Jewish business associate, not kosher. Another faux pas would be giving wine to someone who is either alcoholic or doesn't drink at all.

So what is safe to give someone as a business gift? Again, just keep in mind what the perceived value is in the culture of the person you are gifting. For example, a person from Mexico would think lowly of a gift of silver because it is cheap and abundant there. Chocolate is a gift that can have two different perceptions. If you give someone chocolate that came from Wal-Mart they may perceive that as cheap, but if you give them expensive imported French chocolate they will consider that thoughtful. Just remember it all depends on the person. Gifts should be for a specific individual based upon what you know or have learned about them.

The amount of the gift depends upon the hierarchy in the company. The higher position a person holds the more expensive the gift should be. Also, be sure to never give similar gifts to all those you are gifting.

≫ 12. 4　Office Gift-giving Etiquette

The holidays should be a time of joy and celebration, but often become a time of stress and frustration for those of us who work and face the prospect of giving or receiving holiday presents. Many questions abound. Should you give all your coworkers a present? What do you do when the boss gives you a present? What is an appropriate gift for a coworker, for the boss? Are gag gifts okay? Do you need to reciprocate when a coworker or boss gives you a present? When and how should you present your gifts to coworkers and bosses?

Here are some basic rules of etiquette for enjoying (and surviving) office gift-giving:

1) **Do** first understand the company policy on gift-giving. The larger the company, the more likely a specific policy.

2) **Do** examine the company's corporate culture for the types of gifts that might be acceptable. A gift for a coworker at Google may not be the same thing you get for a coworker at IBM. Rule of

thumb: the more relaxed the corporate culture, the wider latitude you have in gift choices. **Do** use your common sense and good judgment when making gift choices.

3) **Don't** get a gift for anyone in the office for the sake of making a statement; give gifts to show your appreciation and thanks to the people who helped you the most in the past year. And **don't** ever get something for the boss just to show up your coworkers. (You **don't** want to be seen as a suck-up or brown-noser.)

4) **Do** stay within your (and the office) budget for the gifts, and **don't** go overboard on the gifts, especially for the boss.

5) **Don't** assume the people in your office share your tastes. **Don't** assume the people in your office share your tastes.

6) **Do** spend time and effort to choose thoughtful gifts for each on your office list. And it's best to stick to people's hobbies or favorite activities when thinking of gifts. Another safe category would be a gift for the office, such as a gadget, paperweight, calendar, picture frame, pen and pencil set, etc. A last resort would be a gift card to a favorite retailer.

7) **Don't** even think of gag or other inappropriate gifts. **Don't** give items that are too personal, religious, racial, or sexual. Clothing (especially lingerie), perfume/cologne, handmade, regifted, and alcoholic items are also **don'ts**.

8) **Do** consider gifts that can be shared (with coworkers or family members), such as gourmet food items — especially those in festive tins or boxes. Unusual plants or flowers are another possible **do**.

9) **Don't** feel pressure to run out and buy a gift for the boss if he or she gives you one. But **do** send a thank-you note acknowledging the gift and expressing your gratitude.

10) **Don't** give gifts to coworkers in front of others. Instead, **do** consider having a holiday lunch or high tea and exchanging gifts outside the office. If you can't get out of the office, **do** exchange presents discretely (and perhaps after hours).

11) **Do** include a gift receipt so the recipient can easily exchange the item if necessary.

12) **Do** consider giving donations to charities as gifts, but **do** remember that some people prefer gifts, and **don't** ever use donations to controversial charities as a gift.

13) **Do** wrap your gift and **do** consider adding something extra to make the gift even more special, such as a gift of book with a really distinctive book mark.

14) **Don't** wait until the last minute to shop for your coworkers. Whenever possible, **do** plan in advance for the most thoughtful presents.

15) **Do** remember all these rules to have the most success (and joy) when considering office gifts.

≫ 12. 5 **International Gift-giving Etiquette**

Within the interdependent, global and multi-cultural marketplace of the 21st century, cross-cultural differences in the approaches to and practices of business people across the world are important to learn.

A lack of cross-cultural understanding can lead to misunderstandings which may result in offense. Cross-cultural awareness and an understanding of foreign etiquette is important for today's globe trotting business person.

One area of importance in cross-cultural awareness is in the different gift-giving etiquettes of the world. Understanding gift-giving and the etiquette surrounding it can help international business people cement better relationships with foreign colleagues, clients or customers.

Cross-cultural gift-giving etiquette involves considering the following points:

● Who is receiving the gift? Is it a person or a group?
● What is the status of the receiver(s)?
● What types of gifts are acceptable or unacceptable?
● What is the protocol associated with gift-giving and receiving?
● Should gifts be reciprocated?

In order to highlight some of the different aspects of cross-cultural gift-giving etiquette a few examples shall be presented.

1) Gift-giving Etiquette in Japan

● Gift-giving is a central part of Japanese business etiquette.
● Bring a range of gifts for your trip so if you are presented with a gift you will be able to reciprocate.
● The emphasis in Japanese business culture is on the act of gift-giving not the gift itself.
● Expensive gifts are common.
● The best time to present a gift is at the end of your visit.
● A gift for an individual should be given in private.
● If you are presenting a gift to a group of people have them all present.
● The correct etiquette is to present/receive gifts with both hands.
● Before accepting a gift it is polite to refuse at least once or twice before accepting.
● Giving four or nine of anything is considered unlucky. Give in pairs if possible.

2) Gift-giving Etiquette in Saudi Arabia

● Gifts should only be given to the most intimate of friends.
● Gifts should be of the highest quality.
● Never buy gold or silk as a present for men.
● Silver is acceptable.
● Always give/receive gifts with the right hand.
● Saudis enjoy wearing scent-"itr". The most popular is "oud" which can cost as much as £1,000 an ounce.

● It is not bad etiquette to open gifts when received.

3) Gift-giving in Germany

● Gifts are expected for social events, especially to express your thanks after you have been invited to a dinner party at a home.

● Avoid selecting anything obviously expensive, as this may make the other person feel "obligated" to your generosity.

● A lovely bouquet of flowers (though not red roses) for the lady of the house is a typical gift. When purchasing this at the flower shop, ask the florist to wrap it up as a gift.

● For the company you are visiting, quality pens, tasteful office items with your company logo, or imported liquor are usually safe choices.

● Fine chocolates can also be an appropriate gift when you are invited to a home.

● An elegant, tasteful silk scarf can be an acceptable gift for the lady of the house.

● Avoid bringing beer as a gift, since many of the finest brands in the world are already produced and widely available here.

● A small gift is polite, especially when contacts are made for the first time.

● Substantial gifts are not usual, and certainly not before a deal has been reached if you don't want your intentions to be misinterpreted.

● Clothing, perfumes, and other toiletries are considered far too personal to be appropriate gifts. Scarves, however, are acceptable gifts according to German business protocol.

The above are a few of many examples of cross-cultural differences in gift-giving etiquette. It is advisable to try and ascertain some facts about the gift-giving etiquette of any country you plan to visit on business. By doing so, you maximize the potential of your cross cultural encounter.

≫ 12. 6   Gift-giving Etiquette in China

You may think that the beautifully wrapped box you're about to present to your host is a thoughtful gesture, something that will be appreciated, perhaps even cherished. But under the right circumstances, your gift may, in fact, may be an insult tied up in a bow.

In China, as in Minnesota, gifts are often given to express gratitude or friendship or hospitality. It's a common courtesy observed in many cultures.

However, in a business setting, gift-giving is generally frowned upon as a suggestion of bribery. Though this is not always the case, it's important to be proper and properly sensitive when choosing to give a gift in a business context.

For thousands of years, Chinese people have believed that courtesy demands reciprocity, meaning that well-mannered people return favors and kindness. Whenever someone receives a present, treat or invitation from a friend, they will try to offer one back on a suitable occasion. This customary reciprocity is considered necessary to build friendship between people.

Suitable occasions to give gifts include birthdays or wedding days, or for a special holiday or party. Often gifts are also given as a way of saying thank you. Just as anywhere else in the world, what you give depends on how well you know the recipient. And the ideal gift needn't be big or expensive. It should, however, be something that the recipient would appreciate.

1) General Gift-giving Rules

Here are some general rules for giving gifts in a Chinese way:

● Give gifts to people you visit, as a way to thank them for inviting you.

● When giving a "visiting" gift, find something the whole family can use. For example, give food or tea. Or, give something that is important in your home country or community. For example, you might give wild rice from Minnesota or a framed photo of your family.

● In China, tradition dictates that the recipient not appear greedy. Therefore, he or she will often decline a gift two or three times before accepting. If you're the giver, offer again until it is accepted after the third time. At the same time, especially in business, your gift may be absolutely refused, so don't press beyond several refusals.

● Don't be offended if the person does not open the gift in front of you. Chinese people do not usually open a gift in front of the giver. It might embarrass them. They will open it later, then call or write to thank the person for the gift.

● Wrap the gift well. Do not leave the gift in the store's bag. Use colored ribbons to wrap a gift using these colors:
   a. Red for general and happy occasions.
   b. Black and white for funerals.
   c. Gold and silver for wedding gifts.

2) Business Gifts

● In business, show sensitivity to people's status. Give the same type of gift to people at the same level. Or present a gift to a company or organization instead of one person. Giving a gift only to an individual is not acceptable unless it is being given in private as a gesture of friendship.

● Be sure the value of the gift is not extravagant.

● Unless it's a symbolic event, don't photograph the event of giving a gift.

● If negotiations are involved, gifts should be presented once they are finished.

3) Receiving Gifts

Here are some general rules for receiving gifts in a Chinese way:

● Gifts should be received with both hands when presented to you.
● Chinese people who have had contact with Americans or other Westerners might expect you to follow the American custom of opening the gift in front of the giver. To avoid confusion, you can always ask, "Would you like me to open this now?"
● Call or send a thank-you note. And, if possible, offer a gift back on a suitable occasion.

4) Factoids

If you're giving a pen, or signing a card, stay away from red ink. That is a symbol of severing ties. Clocks can symbolize death, and food can connote poverty.

The number 8 is considered lucky, so giving or receiving 8 items is a good thing. Just avoid the number four, which in Cantonese, is a lot like the word for death.

≫　12. 7　Some Tips for Gift-giving

1) Motive, Relationship, and Money

Before trying to decide on the right gift for someone at work you should first consider three very important things: Motive, Relationship, and Money.

a. Motive

Are you giving because you feel that you have to? If yes, think again. If you give a gift reluctantly, it is likely to show in some way. Instead of giving a cheap or thoughtless gift because your heart (or pocket book) is not in it, give a gift card or greeting card instead.

b. Relationship

What is the relationship you have with the person you are giving a gift to? Is it purely professional or a combination of friendship and professional? The more formal your relationship, the more formal the gift should be (and less reason to give one in the first place). Gifts should honor existing relationships, not be given as a way to create them.

c. Money

You do not have to spend a lot of money on any one gift (in fact, business etiquette does not require you to give a gift to anyone in the workplace), but will giving to one person create a situation where you will then need to give to others as well? And, even a ten dollar gift can still be a financial hardship for many people.

If you cannot afford to give gifts, don't, but do not apologize of making excuses for not giving gifts. Treating others with respect and appreciation throughout the entire year is gift enough.

2) Proper Gift-giving Etiquette for Health and Fitness

It's easy to overlook proper gift-giving etiquette. Let's face it, We usually have other things on our minds. Sometimes we struggle forever deciding on the perfect gift for a friend or family member. Other times an idea pops into our head quickly, and we're convinced the idea is so perfect that we fail to question the decision further. That's often the case when it comes to fitness equipment and health and exercise gifts.

a. Healthy and Fitness

This is a sensitive topic. Giving health-related gifts or exercise equipment isn't always easy. Basically, there are certain people you can give these types of gifts to and certain people you should never consider giving such gifts to. Below you'll learn a little more about how to tell the difference.

b. What's Your Relationship

If your spouse, or friend, or relative hints at exercise gear or a new diet book as a gift choice, then it's certainly acceptable for you to give such a gift. You wouldn't give this type of gift to your child's teacher or a casual acquaintance, though you really should refrain from giving exercise or diet related gifts to anyone you're not particularly close with. The items are just too personal, and you really don't want anyone thinking that you think it's time they got off the couch or cut junk food from their diet.

c. Don't Forget Yourself

The perfect person to give exercise and health-related gifts to is you! If you see a new exercise gadget or want a new warm-up suit, go ahead and indulge. Any exercise-related "gift" to yourself is well worth it if it keeps you motivated to stay fit and eat healthy. The best benefit is that you won't be violating any proper gift-giving etiquette when you reward yourself with something special.

≫ 12.8 Skills and Strategies

1) Choosing Gift

(1) Does he have some special hobbies? Such as drinking tea or wine, collecting stamps or Chinese calligraphy, etc. ?

(2) But Americans can buy Chinese tea there in America. You know we export a lot to them.

(3) But the fact that you choose it and bring it all the way from China with you makes it very special.

(4) If you want to bring something, it should be small inexpensive item. You could bring some candy or toys for the kids or something special from China. But better not the things on

which printed your company's name for personal friends.

(5) I don't know what gift I should bring with me. You could bring some post cards of Chinese scenery or bookmarks or things like that.

2) Sending gifts

(1) This gift is for you and your wife.

(2) Here is a little something for you. I hope you'll like it.

(3) Please accept this gift. It's a token of your friendship.

(4) I'm so pleased that you like it.

(5) I'm so happy you like.

3) Accepting gifts

(1) It's really nice. I'll always think of you when I see this.

(2) Thank you very much. You are very thoughtful. You know, chocolates are my favorite.

(3) Well, the gift is really a surprise. It's very kind of you.

(4) Oh, it's very kind of you. How beautiful it is! Shall I open it now?

(5) It looks so cute. I'll keep it in my bedroom.

(6) It is not only beautiful but also practical.

4) Special gifts

(1) On behalf of our company, I'd like to present you a gift, Mr. Smith, It's a sample violin for you from our America branch.

(2) It was very kind of you to have given me such a special gift. I hope we'll cooperative well this time. Thanks again.

(3) It would be the best that we can obtain the quality index.

(4) Oh, thank you! It's very kind of you. This is exactly what I want. Ah, it's quite novel for us.

(5) Yes, I like it very much. It's more new model and I think it can help us to develop more new products. Thank you very much for such a good present.

(6) This gift will help to improve the quality of our production. Thank you very much.

Business Etiquette in Europe

>>> 1. Some Basic Etiquette in Europe

Europe ranges from the cold northern countries of Norway and Sweden to the warm Mediterranean countries of Italy and Greece. Some customs vary as much as the topography, while others are shared across all of Europe.

Handshakes

Handshakes are standard business greeting gestures throughout Europe. However, the European handshake is usually exchanged before and after every meeting, no matter how many meetings you've already had. An exception is Great Britain, where, as in the United States, an initial handshake is often the only one you'll receive.

European handshakes are more formal and less buddy-buddy than those in the United States. You will not find a lot of back-slapping at handshaking time. A quick grasp and release is the norm. In most European countries, handshakes are firm. An exception is France, where a lighter grasp is customary.

Finally, it's customary to let women and those in a higher rank to extend their hands first in Europe.

Names and Titles

It's unusual in Europe for people to use first names immediately. Wait until he asks you to call him by his first name or uses a familiar form of address with you.

Titles, especially academic titles, are always used in Europe. In the United States, it's unusual for a Professor to be called *Doctor* or *Professor* outside of the classroom, but in European countries, professors, along with lawyers, medical doctors, and others are introduced with their title(s).

Dining and Entertaining

Europeans don't do business breakfasts. In France, Austria, Germany, Great Britain, the Netherlands, Norway, Denmark, Sweden, Finland, Portugal, and Spain, talking business over lunch is not a violation of etiquette. In the Czech Republic, Italy, and Greece, on the other hand, you do not talk business over lunch unless your host initiates it.

Dinner in Europe is usually reserved for social entertaining. Depending on the country, you may start dinner as early as 6:30 p. m. or as late as 11:00 p. m. Depending on the country your spouse may be invited.

Dining is taken seriously in most of Europe as an expression of generosity. In some countries, such as Italy and Greece, this generosity can reach stupefying levels; it can be virtually impossible to pick up a check in Italy and virtually impossible not to overeat or overdrink in Greece. But it's rude to refuse dinner invitations or any of the sumptuous items proffered to you at a dinner.

Here are some general dining rules:

- In Norway, Sweden, Finland, Denmark, be on time for dinner. Elsewhere, being fashionably late is acceptable.
- No host gift is expected in Great Britain.
- Do not take wine to a dinner in The Netherlands, France, or Belgium. It insinuates that you think the host's cellar is lacking.

Gifts giving

In some countries, for instance, a small host gift is appropriate if you are invited to someone's home for dinner. But not in Great Britain — here, no host gift is expected.

Across most of Europe, business gifts should not be too personal and should be wrapped professionally. Try not to use white wrapping paper, and use a brightly color ribbon.

Social Taboos

In many European countries, asking people what they do or asking them a personal question as an opening conversational gambit is a serious mistake. Europeans are, for the most part, more formal and reserved about such matters than Americans are. Watch out for these gesture-related mistakes:

- The American gesture for "OK" using a circle formed by forefinger and thumb is offensive in Germany.
- Showing your palm to someone is offensive in Greece.
- Keeping your hands in your pockets is rude.
- Back-slapping is out of place in northern Europe.
- Having your hands below the table while dining in France, Germany, and Austria is rude.

≫≫ 2. Business Etiquettes in the United Kingdom

England is one of four distinct regions of the United Kingdom, which also includes Wales, Scotland, and Northern Ireland. England's population is approximately 47 million.

It is important to note that the Scots, Welsh, and Irish are not English, and are often offended when referred to as such. Additionally, citizens of the U. K. do not consider themselves European. Unfortunately, they are usually grouped as such, due in part to their membership in the European Union.

Dress Etiquette

Business attire rules are somewhat relaxed in England, but conservative dress is still very important for both men and women. Dark suits, usually black, blue, or gray, are quite acceptable. Men's shirts should not have pockets; if they do, the pockets should always be kept empty. Additionally, men should wear solid or patterned ties, while avoiding striped ties. Men wear laced shoes, not loafers. Businesswomen are not as limited to colors and styles as men are, though it is still important to maintain a conservative image.

Socializing Etiquette

Always be punctual in England. Arriving a few minutes early for safety is acceptable.

Decision-making is slower in England than in the United States; therefore it is unwise to rush the English into making a decision.

A simple handshake is the standard greeting (for both men and women) for business occasions and for visiting a home.

Privacy is very important to the English. Therefore asking personal questions or intensely staring at another person should be avoided. Eye contact is seldom kept during British conversations.

To signal that something is to be kept confidential or secret, tap your nose. Personal space is important in England, and one should maintain a wide physical space when conversing. Furthermore, it is considered inappropriate to touch others in public. Gifts are generally not part of doing business in England.

A business lunch will often be conducted in a pub and will consist of a light meal and perhaps a pint of ale. When socializing after work hours, do not bring up the subject of work. When dining out, it is not considered polite to toast those who are older than yourself.

Communications

George Bernard once said: "America and Britain are two nations divided by a common language". In England, English is the official language, but it should be noted that Queen's English and American English are very different. Often times ordinary vocabulary can differ between the two countries.

Loud talking and disruptive behavior should be avoided. One gesture to avoid is the V for Victory sign, done with the palm facing yourself. This is a very offensive gesture. If a man has been knighted, he is addressed as "Sir and His First Name", example: Sir John. If writing a letter, the envelope is addressed "Sir First name and Last name", example: Sir John Roberts.

Business Meetings

Meetings can sometimes appear rather anarchic with little apparent structure or direction. This is in keeping with Britain's proud democratic tradition that allows everyone his or her say, but it can also be misleading. While teamwork is important, British business culture remains essentially hierarchical. A wide range of input is valued and a consensus may be reached but the final decision still rests with the most powerful (usually, but not always, the most senior) individual who may or may not be chairing any given meeting.

≫ 3. Business Etiquette in France

French business behavior emphasizes courtesy and a degree of formality. Mutual trust and respect is required to get things done. Trust is earned through proper behavior. Creating a wide network of close personal business alliances is very important. If you do not speak French, an apology for not knowing their language may aid in developing a relationship.

It is always a good idea to learn a few key phrases, since it demonstrates an interest in a long-term relationship. The way a French person communicates is often predicated by their social status, education level, and which part of the country they were raised.

In business, the French often appear extremely direct because they are not afraid of asking probing questions. Written communication is formal. Secretaries often schedule meetings and may be used to relay information from your French business colleagues.

Meeting Etiquette

The handshake is a common form of greeting. Friends may greet each other by lightly kissing on the cheeks, once on the left cheek and once on the right cheek. First names are reserved for family and close friends. Wait until invited before using someone's first name. You are expected to say "bonjour" or "bonsoir" (good morning and good evening) with the honorific title Monsieur or Madame when entering a shop and "au revoir" (good-bye) when leaving. If you live in an apartment building, it is polite to greet your neighbors with the same appellation.

Gift-giving Etiquette

Flowers should be given in odd numbers but not 13, which is considered unlucky. Some older French retain old-style prohibitions against receiving certain flowers: White lilies or chrysanthemums as they are used at funerals; red carnations as they symbolize bad will; any white flowers as they are used at weddings.

Prohibitions about flowers are not generally followed by the young. When in doubt, it is always best to err on the side of conservatism. If you give wine, make sure it is of the highest quality you can afford. The French appreciate their wines. Gifts are usually opened when received.

Dining Etiquette

If you are invited to a French house for dinner, remember:

● Arrive on time. Under no circumstances should you arrive more than 10 minutes later than invited without telephoning to explain you have been detained.
● The further south you go in the country, the more flexible time is.
● If invited to a large dinner party, especially in Paris, send flowers the morning of the occasion so that they may be displayed that evening.
● Dress well. The French are fashion conscious and their version of casual is not as relaxed as in many western countries.

Table Manners

Table manners are Continental — the fork is held in the left hand and the knife in the right while eating. If there is a seating plan, you may be directed to a particular seat. Do not begin eating until the hostess says "bon appetit". If you have not finished eating, cross your knife and fork on your plate with the fork over the knife. Do not rest your elbows on the table, although your hands should be visible and not in your lap. Finish everything on your plate. Do not cut salad with a knife and fork. Fold the lettuce on to your fork. Peel and slice fruit before eating it. Leave your wineglass nearly full if you do not want more.

Business Meetings Etiquette

Appointments are necessary and should be made at least 2 weeks in advance. Appointments may be made in writing or by telephone and, depending upon the level of the person you are meeting, are often handled by the secretary. Do not try to schedule meetings during July or August, as this is a common vacation period.

If you expect to be delayed, telephone immediately and offer an explanation. Do not try to schedule meetings during July or August, as this is a common vacation period. Meetings are to discuss issues, not to make decisions. Avoid exaggerated claims, as the French do not appreciate hyperbole.

Business Negotiation

French business emphasizes courtesy and a fair degree of formality. You will have to wait to be told where to sit and maintain direct eye contact while speaking. Business is conducted slowly. You will have to be patient and not appear ruffled by the strict adherence to protocol. Avoid confrontational behavior or high-pressure tactics. It can be counter-productive.

The French will carefully analyze every detail of a proposal, regardless of how minute. Business is hierarchical. Decisions are generally made at the top of the company. The French are often impressed with good debating skills that demonstrate an intellectual grasp of the situation and all the ramifications.

Never attempt to be overly friendly. The French generally compartmentalize their business and personal lives. Discussions may be heated and intense. High-pressure sales tactics should be avoided. The French are more receptive to a low-key, logical presentation that explains the advantages of a proposal in full.

When an agreement is reached, the French may insist it be formalized in an extremely comprehensive, precisely worded contract. When an agreement is reached, the French may insist it be formalized in an extremely comprehensive, precisely worded contract.

Dress Etiquation

Business dress is understated and stylish. Men should wear dark-colored, conservative business suits for the initial meeting. How you dress later is largely dependent upon the personality of the company with which you are conducting business. Women should wear either business suits or elegant dresses in soft colors. The French like the finer things in life, so wear good quality accessories.

Business Cards

Business cards are exchanged after the initial introductions without formal ritual. Have the other side of your business card translated into French. Although not a business necessity, it demonstrates an attention to detail that will be appreciated. Include any advanced academic degrees on your business card. French business cards are often a bit larger than in many other countries.

≫ 4. Business Etiquette inItaly

Italians prefer to do business with people they know and trust. A third party introduction will go a long way in providing an initial platform from which to work. Italians much prefer face-to-face contact, so it is important to spend time in Italy developing the relationship.

Your business colleagues will be eager to know something about you as a person before conducting business with you. Demeanor is important as Italians judge people on appearances and the first impression you make will be a lasting one. Italians are intuitive. Therefore, make an effort to ensure that your Italians colleagues like and trust you.

Networking can be an almost full-time occupation in Italy. Personal contacts allow people to get ahead. You have to take the time to ask questions about your business colleagues family and personal interests, as this helps build the relationship. Italians are extremely expressive communicators. They tend to be wordy, eloquent, emotional, and demonstrative, often using facial and hand gestures to prove their point.

Meeting Etiquette

Greetings are enthusiastic yet rather formal. The usual handshake with direct eye contact and a smile suffices between strangers. Once a relationship develops, air-kissing on both cheeks, starting with the left is often added as well as a pat on the back between men. Wait until invited to move to a first name basis. Wait until invited to move to a first name basis.

Italians are guided by first impressions, so it is important that you demonstrate propriety and respect when greeting people, especially when meeting them for the first time. Many Italians use calling cards in social situations. These are slightly larger than traditional business cards and include the person's name, address, title or academic honors, and their telephone number.

If you are staying in Italy for an extended period of time, it is a good idea to have calling cards made. Never give your business card in lieu of a calling card in a social situation.

Gift-giving Etiquette

InItaly, if you would like to send gifts to business counterparts, please bear the following tips in your mind:
- Do not give chrysanthemums as they are used at funerals.
- Do notgive red flowers as they indicate secrecy.
- Do not give yellow flowers as they indicate jealousy.
- If you bring wine, make sure it is a good vintage. Quality, rather than quantity, is important.
- Do not wrap gifts in black, as is traditionally a mourning color.
- Do not wrap gifts in purple, as it is a symbol of bad luck.
- Gifts are usually opened when received.

Dining Etiquette

If you are invited to Italian house, and invitation says the dress is informal, wear stylish clothes that are still rather formal, i. e. , jacket and tie for men and an elegant dress for women.

Punctuality is not mandatory. You may arrive between 15 minutes late if invited to dinner and up to 30 minutes late if invited to a party.

If you are invited to a meal, bring gift-wrapped such as wine or chocolates. If you are invited for dinner and want to send flowers, have them delivered that day. Please remember:

● Remain standing until invited to sit down. You may be shown to a particular seat. Table manners are Continental — the fork is held in the left hand and the knife in the right while eating.

● Follow the lead of the hostess — she sits at the table first, starts eating first, and is the first to get up at the end of the meal. The host gives the first toast. An honored guest should return the toast later in the meal. Women may offer a toast.

● Always take a small amount at first so you can be cajoled into accepting a second helping. Do not keep your hands in your lap during the meal; however, do not rest your elbows on the table either.

● It is acceptable to leave a small amount of food on your plate. Pick up cheese with your knife rather than your fingers. If you do not want more wine, leave your wineglass nearly full.

Business Meeting Etiquette

Appointments are mandatory and should be made in writing (in Italian) 2 to 3 weeks in advance. Reconfirm the meeting by telephone or fax. Many companies are closed in August, and if they are open many Italians take vacations at this time, so it is best not to try to schedule meetings then. In the north, punctuality is viewed as a virtue and your business associates will most likely be on time.

In the north, punctuality is viewed as a virtue and your business associates will most likely be on time. The goal of the initial meeting is to develop a sense of respect and trust with your Italian business colleagues. Have all your printed material available in both English and Italian, and hire an interpreter if you are not fluent in Italian.

It is common to be interrupted while speaking or for several people to speak at once. People often raise their voice to be heard over other speakers, not because they are angry.

Although written agendas are frequently provided, they may not be followed. They serve as a jumping off point for further discussions. Decisions are not reached in meetings. Meetings are meant for a free flow of ideas and to let everyone have their say. Decisions are not reached in meetings.

Business Negotiation

In the north, people are direct, see time as money, and get down to business after only a brief period of social talk. In the south, people take a more leisurely approach to life and want to get to know the people with whom they do business. You will have to allow your Italian business colleagues to set the pace for your negotiations. Follow their lead as to when it is appropriate to move from social to business discussions.

Italians prefer to do business with high-ranking people. Hierarchy is the cornerstone of Italian business. Italians respect power and age. Business Etiquette and Protocol in Italy

Negotiations are often protracted. Italians never use high-pressure sales tactics and they always adhere to your verbal agreements. Failing to follow through on a commitment will destroy a business relationship.

Debates and arguments often erupt in meetings. This is simply a function of the free-flow of ideas. Haggling over price and delivery date is common. Decisions are often based more on how you are viewed by the other party than on concrete business objectives.

Dress Etiquette

Dressing well is a priority in Italy. Men should wear dark colored, conservative business suits. Women should wear either business suits or conservative dresses. Elegant accessories are equally important for men and women. Elegant accessories are equally important for men and women.

Business Cards

Business cards are exchanged after the formal introduction. Business cards are exchanged after the formal introduction. To demonstrate proper respect for the other person, look closely at their business card before putting it in your card holder. It is a good idea to have one side of your business card translated into Italian. If you have a graduate degree, include it on your business card. Make sure your title is on your card. Italians like knowing how you fit within your organization.

≫ 5. Business Etiquette in Spain

The Spanish prefer to do business with those they know and trust. It is important that you spend sufficient time letting your business colleagues get to know you. Once you develop a relationship, it will prevail even if you switch companies, since your Spanish business colleagues' allegiance will be to you rather than the company you represent.

Communication

Face-to-face contact is preferred to written or telephone communication. The way you present yourself is of critical importance when dealing with Spaniards. It is best to display modesty when describing your achievements and accomplishments.

Communication is formal and follows rules of protocol. Avoid confrontation if at all possible. Spaniards do not like to publicly admit that they are incorrect. Trust and personal relationships are the cornerstone of business. Spaniards, like many societies, are concerned that they look good in the eyes of others and try to avoid looking foolish at all times.

Meeting Etiquette

When you are introduced, you will expect to shake hands. Once a relationship is established, men may embrace and pat each other on the shoulder. Female friends kiss each other on both cheeks, starting with the left. People are often referred to as Don or Dona and their first name when in formal occasion as a general rule. Many men use a two-handed shake where the left hand is placed on the right forearm of the other person.

Dinning Etiquette

If you are invited to a Spaniard's home, you can bring chocolates, pastries, or cakes; wine, liqueur, or brandy; or flowers to the hostess. If you know your hosts have children, they may be included in the evening, so a small gift for them is always appreciated.

When you are invited to a meal, remain standing until invited to sit down. You may be shown to a particular seat. You will have to keep your hands visible when eating and keep your wrists resting on the edge of the table. Remember:

- Do not begin eating until the hostess starts.
- Use utensils to eat most food. Even fruit is eaten with a knife and fork.
- If you have not finished eating, cross your knife and fork on your plate with the fork over the knife.
- The host gives the first toast. An honored guest should return the toast later in the meal. It is acceptable for a woman to make a toast.
- Indicate you have finished eating by laying your knife and fork parallel on your plate, tines facing up, with the handles facing to the right.
- Do not get up until the guest of honor does.

Business Negotiation

Spaniards place great importance on the character of the person with whom they do business.

Hierarchy and rank are important. You should deal with people of similar rank to your own. Decision-making is held at the top of the company, since this is a hierarchical country. You may never actually meet the person who ultimately makes the decision.

You may be interrupted while you are speaking. This is not an insult; it merely means the person is interested in what you are saying. Spaniards do not like to lose face, so they will not necessarily say that they do not understand something, particularly if you are not speaking Spanish. You must be adept at discerning body language.

Spaniards are very thorough. They will review every minute detail to make certain it is understood. First you must reach an oral understanding. A formal contract will be drawn up at a later date. Spaniards expect both sides to strictly adhere to the terms of a contract.

Business Meeting Etiquette

Appointments are mandatory and should be made in advance, preferably by telephone or fax. Reconfirm in writing or by telephone the week before. You should try to arrive on time for meetings.

The first meeting is generally formal and is used to get to know each other. Do not be surprised if no business is actually conducted during the first meeting. The first meeting is generally formal and is used to get to know each other. Do not be surprised if no business is actually conducted during the first meeting. Agendas are often used but not always needed to be followed too strict.

Make sure all your printed material is available in both English and Spanish. Not all businesspeople speak English, so it is wise to check if you should hire an interpreter. Several people may speak at once. You may be interrupted while you are speaking.

Decisions are not reached at meetings. Meetings are for discussion and to exchange ideas. Most Spaniards do not give their opinion at meetings. Therefore, it is important to watch their non-verbal communication.

Dress Etiquette

Business dress is stylish yet, conservative. Dress as you would in the rest of Europe. Elegant accessories are important for both men and women.

Business Cards

Present your business card to the receptionist upon arriving. Have one side of your card translated into Spanish. Hand your card so the Spanish side faces the recipient.

≫ 6. Business Etiquette in Austria

In Austria, First impressions are important and you will be judged on your clothing and demeanor. Although Austrians prefer third-party introductions, they do not need a personal relationship in order to do business. They will be interested in any advanced university degrees you might have as well as the amount of time your company has been in business.

Austrians show deference to people in authority, so it is imperative that they understand your level relative to their own. It is imperative that you exercise good manners in all your business interactions. There is little joking or small talk in the office as they are serious and focused on accomplishing business objectives/goals.

Communication

Communication is formal and follows strict rules of protocol. Always use the formal word for you "sie" unless invited to use the informal "du". Address people by their academic title and surname. You may be referred to simply by your surname. This is not a culture that uses first names except with family and close friends. Austrians are suspicious of hyperbole, promises that sound too good to be true, or displays of emotion. Austrians are suspicious of hyperbole, promises that sound too good to be true, or displays of emotion.

In many situations, Austrians will be direct to the point of bluntness. This is not an attempt to be rude, it is simply indicative of their desire to move the discussion along.

You will expect a great deal of written communication, both to back up decisions and to maintain a record of discussions and outcomes.

Meeting Etiquette

Greetings are formal. A quick, firm handshake is the traditional greeting. Austrians maintain eye contact during the greeting. Some Austrian men, particularly those who are older, may kiss the hand of a female.

A male from another country should not kiss an Austrian woman's hand. Women may also kiss men, but men never kiss other men.

Titles are very important and denote respect. Use a person's title and their surname until invited to use their first name. When entering a room, shake hands with everyone individually, including children.

Gift-giving Etiquette

In general, Austrians exchange gifts with family and close friends at Christmas (generally Christmas Eve) and birthdays. Children receive gifts on December 6th, the feast of St. Nicholas.

If invited to dinner at an Austrian's house, bring a small gift of consumables such as chocolates. If giving flowers, always give an odd number as except for 12, even numbers mean bad luck. Do not give red carnations, lilies, or chrysanthemums. Gifts should be nicely wrapped. Gifts are usually opened when received.

Dinning Etiquette

If you are invited to an Austrian's house:
● Arrive on time. Punctuality is a sign of respect.
● Dress conservatively and elegantly.
● In some houses you may be asked to remove your shoes, although the custom is not as prevalent as it once was.
● Remain standing until invited to sit down. You may be shown to a particular seat.

Table manners are Continental — the fork is held in the left hand and the knife in the right while eating. Watch your table manners:

- Put your napkin on your lap as soon as you sit down.
- Do not begin eating until the hostess says "mahlzeit" or "Guten Appetit".
- Cut as much of your food with your fork as possible, since this compliments the cook by saying the food is very tender.
- Finish everything on your plate.
- Indicate you have finished eating by laying your knife and fork parallel on your plate with the handles facing to the right.
- The host gives the first toast. Everyone lifts and clinks glasses, looks the person making the toast in the eye and says, "Prost!".
- An honored guest offers a toast of thanks to the host at the end of the meal.

Business Meeting Etiquette

Appointments are necessary and should be made 3 to 4 weeks in advance when meeting with private companies. Do not try to schedule meetings in August, the two weeks surrounding Christmas, or the week before Easter. Punctuality is taken extremely seriously. If you expect to be delayed, telephone immediately and offer an explanation. It is extremely rude to cancel a meeting at the last minute and it could ruin your business relationship.

Meetings are formal. Presentations should be accurate and precise. Have back-up material and be prepared to defend everything: Austrians are meticulous about details. Meetings adhere to strict agendas, including starting and ending times. If you have an agenda, it will be followed

Follow-up with a letter outlining what was agreed, what the next steps are, and who is the responsible party.

Business Negotiation

Do not sit until invited and told where to sit. There is a rigid protocol to be followed. Meetings adhere to strict agendas, including starting and ending times. A small amount of getting-to-know-you conversation may take place before the business conversation begins. Austrians are more concerned with long-term relationships than making a quick sale.

Rank and position are important. Since most companies are relatively small, it is often quite easy to meet with the decision-maker. Business is conducted slowly. You will have to be patient and not appear ruffled by the strict adherence to protocol.

Austrians are very detail-oriented and want to understand every innuendo before coming to agreement. Avoid confrontational behavior or high-pressure tactics. It can work against you.

Dress Etiquette

Business dress is conservative and follows most European conventions. Men should wear dark colored, conservative business suits with white shirts. Women should wear either business suits or conservative dresses, complimented with elegant accessories.

Business Cards

Business cards are exchanged without formal ritual. Have one side of your card translated into German. Although not a business necessity, it demonstrates an attention to detail. Include any advanced academic degrees or honors on your business card. If your company has been in business for a long time, include the founding date on your card as it demonstrates stability.

Business Etiquette in Asia

≫ 1. Business Etiquette in Asia

Asia covers China, Japan, Malaysia, Vietnam, South Korea, the Philippines, and other countries in the Pacific. These countries often have radically distinct cultures with radically distinctive etiquette.

Handshakes

When you are in the Asian countries, you can shake hands. But avoid direct eye contact during the handshakes, and do not shake very hard or very long. Your host may bow to you. The more senior you are, the deeper the bow. You may also bow. The bow is a sign of mutual respect.

The Philippines is the exception here. Don't bow, but do make direct eye contact.

Business Cards

The exchange of business cards must be made properly. Business cards should be printed in English on one side and in your host's language on the other. When you present your card, you do so with both hands, native language side up and readable to your host. When you receive a card in return, study it, thank the person, and place the card gently in your jacket pocket.

Meetings

Meetings begin more or less on time in China, Japan, South Korea, Thailand, and in the Chinese population of Indonesia. In Malaysia, Vietnam, and the Philippines, meetings are less likely to start punctually.

In China most of the junior Chinese business associates will arrive early. You do not have to start the meeting ahead of time. They are there in case you need anything.

Business Attire

Your default business wardrobe is conservative business dress, with suits. Ties, and tie-up for men, and conservative suits and dresses for women. Because of their warmer climates, some leniency in dress is to be found in Vietnam, Malaysia, the Philippines, Singapore, and in Hong Kong area. But even in these countries, be conservative and avoid flashiness of any kind.

Dining and Entertaining

Asians love to entertain in bars and restaurants and the food is exquisitely flavored, prepared, and presented.

In China, we often entertain foreign guests with a banquet — long meal with innumerable courses served one after the other. Guests are expected to arrive on time and get ready to eat. Take something from every serving dish, even if it's only a little amount. But never clean your plate symbolically, the magnificence of the meal means that you can't finish it.

In Japan, foreign guests will be hosted to an evening of eating and drinking. Remember: let your host order and enjoy something from each platter. Don't refuse to eat sushi or sashimi — (both of which involve raw fish) — you'll insult your host. Drink your beer or sake slowly — you host will fill your cup every time it's empty.

Koreans entertain both at home and at restaurants. Arrive on time if you're going to a private home, and bring a small gift. If you're invited out to a night on the Town, be appropriately grateful, for your host is probably planning to spend a lot of money.

The Filipinos style of entertaining is to invite you to a private home, where you and a gaggle of your host's friends will enjoy a lavish meal.

⟫ 2. Business Etiquette in Japan

There is heightened sense of formality in Japanese interaction. When doing business in Japan, your suitability in respect to conducting business will be assessed during a first meeting, so always maintain a sense of professionalism.

Meeting and Greeting

The bow is an integral part of Japanese society. It is used when meeting, getting attention, to show gratitude, to express sympathy or as an apology. Whilst doing business in Japan as a Westerner, you would not be expected to bow. You will most likely be greeted with a handshake combined with a slight nod of the head.

Introduce yourself with your full name followed by your company name. It is important to use proper titles when addressing someone, so always establish the position of the other person.

The exchanging of business cards when doing business in Japan involves a degree of ceremony. The card is seen to represent the individual, so should be treated with respect. Before traveling to Japan, ensure you have ample cards and have one side translated into Japanese. Include your position within the company on it. Invest in a carry case to store cards and keep this in the inside pocket of a suit jacket.

When exchanging, offer your card with both hands or just the right hand. Present Japanese side up. Ensure there is no barrier between you and the recipient such as a table, chair or plant. When accepting always use two hands as this shows deference.

Building Relationship

Introduce yourself with your full name followed by your company name. It is important to use proper titles when addressing someone, so always establish the position of the other person. Introduce yourself with your full name followed by your company name. It is important to use proper titles when addressing someone, so always establish the position of the other person.

When doing business in Japan a successful relationship with a Japanese colleague or client is based on three factors: sincerity, compatibility and trustworthiness. Sincerity means that you are compromising, understanding and you want to conduct business on a personal level. Compatibility is established when you are seen to be concerned about the personal relationship, the well-being of the company and not just focused on financial gain. Trustworthiness relates to the faith put in you to protect from loss face.

Communication

The emphasis in Japanese culture on maintaining harmony has developed in such a way as to allow very vague forms of expression. The cultural logic behind this is that by avoiding direct or explicit statements one has a better chance of not causing offense.

When doing business in Japan clarify meanings and dig deeper for more information. The Japanese are implicit communicators. An explicit communicator assumes the listener is unaware of background information or related issues to the topic of discussion and provides it themselves. The Japanese however assume the listener is well informed on the subject and minimizes information relayed on the premise that listener will understand from implication. Thus the saying, "Say one, understand ten," i. e., you will be expected to understand nine additional points to every one made.

Meetings and Negotiations

At a meeting you will always deal with a team as opposed to an individual. Each attendee will be there with a particular expertise so either bring assistance or be sure you are confident enough to handle all the questions you will receive.

You will greet the most senior employee first and then others in descending order. The senior employee will be there as a ceremonial representative of the company. The lesser ranking attendees will usually do the talking or negotiating.

Meetings usually take place for only one of three reasons: to build rapport, exchange information or confirm previously made decisions. Decisions are rarely made in a meeting.

If rapport has yet to be established, then this is your priority. It is important not only to build relationships with all the senior figures but all lower ranked ones too. Remember group consensus is important so the opinions of all staff will be taken into account when coming to a decision on any proposal.

The Japanese are very detail orientated. Expect lots of questions and lots of questions repeated in different ways. Be sure to have the answers as the failure to do so will look unprofessional. Be sure to bring as much information as possible, in writing, on your company, service, product or proposal.

The Japanese like dealing with quiet, sincere and compromising individuals. Extroverts are seen as brash and arrogant. Early on in negotiations remain humble, indirect and non-threatening. Do not disagree openly, do not put people on the spot and always employ diplomatic language when doing business. Be sure to hold off concessions till the end of proceedings. If made early your integrity will be questioned.

Silence is considered a virtue. If things go quiet when doing business in a meeting, then do not panic. Reflection is taking place. Silence may be also be accompanied by the closing of the eyes. Never interrupt or break the silence.

≫ 3. Business Etiquette in South Korea

Despite outside influences from its neighboring countries, South Korea has maintained a distinct and homogeneous identity influenced by its religious beliefs and breathtaking landscapes. The people of Korea share a common pride in the country's unique cultural and linguistic heritage that has emerged during her long and turbulent history. As a result, Korea boasts an enriched cultural outlook that is reflected in its current business culture.

Personal Relationships

In Korea, personal relations take precedence over business. In order to be successful, it is vital to establish good, personal relationships based on mutual trust and benefit. Korean business culture is firmly grounded in respectful rapport and in order to establish this, it is essential that you have the right introduction and approach the company through a mutual friend or acquaintance at the appropriate level. Koreans spend a significant amount of time developing and fostering personal contacts. Therefore, time should be allocated for this process, particularly during the first meeting, which is frequently used to simply establish rapport and build trust. Once good, solid relations have been recognized in Korea, continuous reinforcement and maintenance is vital.

Doing Business with Koreans

The changing face of Korea continues to evolve at an unprecedented pace in current Korean society. A country well known for its difficult history, Korea was liberated from Japanese occupation at the end of World War Ⅱ, only to be faced with the Cold War struggle that divided the country into two separate states; the Southern democratic republic, and the Northern communist style government. In the years that followed the Korean War, South Korea experienced rapid economic development and has continued to prosper in today's modern world economy, becoming the largest in Asia after Japan and China. The present-day increase in business opportunities in Korea only increases the importance of cultural knowledge for those wishing to enter into this modern day market.

Working Practices

Before doing business in Korea prior appointments are required and should generally be made a few weeks in advance. The most suitable times to arrange a business meeting are normally between 10 a. m. and 12 p. m. or 2 p. m. and 4 p. m.

For both social occasions and business meetings, punctuality is essential. Your Korean counterparts will expect you to arrive on time as a sign of respect; therefore it is advised to call beforehand if you will be delayed. You may find however, that top Korean business executives may arrive a few minutes late to appointments. This is a reflection of their extremely busy and pressured schedule and should not be taken with offence.

It is recommended that you send any proposals, company brochures, and marketing material, written in both Korean and English, as a preview for your Korean contacts before you visit the country.

Structure and Hierarchy in Korean Companies

Korea is known for its vertical social structure based on age and social status. The organizational arrangement of Korean companies is highly centralized with authority concentrated in senior levels. Korea is known for its vertical social structure based on age and social status. The organizational arrangement of Korean companies is highly centralized with authority concentrated in senior levels.

Influenced by Confucianism, Koreans respect for authority is paramount in their business culture and practices. High-ranking individuals tend to have more power over their subordinates than in the West. Consequently, decision making in Korea will follow a formal procedure in which senior approval is necessary.

Working Relationships in Korea

Generally speaking, responsibility is delegated to trusted, dependable subordinates by their superiors. Therefore, it is imperative not to offend or ignore the lower ranks and to show the various managers the same respect as other senior levels.

Age is the most essential component within a relationship in Korea. A person older than you automatically holds a certain level of superiority. This is particularly evident in Korean business settings.

Personal ties in Korea, such as kinship, schools, birthplaces, etc., often take precedence over job seniority, rank or other factors, and have significant influence over the structure and management of Korean companies. significant influence over the structure and management of Korean companies.

Business Practices in Korea

The exchange of business cards in Korea is vital for initiating introductions. Korean's prefer to know the person they are dealing with. Therefore, it is important to emphasize your title so that the correct authority, status, and rank is established. It is advised to have the reverse side of your card translated into Korean. Cards should be presented and accepted with both hands and must be read and studied with respect and consideration before placing them on the table.

Gift-giving is a common practice within Korean business settings. Generally given at the first business meeting, gifts are often used to acquire favours and build relationships. You should allow the host to present his gift first and be sure to accept the gift with both hands. To avoid loss of face, gifts of similar value should be exchanged and gifts of greater value should be given to the most senior person respectively.

Like most Asian countries, Koreans believe that contracts are a starting point, rather than the final stage of a business agreement and prefer them to be left flexible enough so that adjustments can be made. Although many Koreans now appreciate the legal implications regarding the signing of contracts, they may still be interpreted as less important than the interpersonal relationship established between the two companies. It is vital that you are aware of how your Korean counterparts view these documents in order to avoid any possible misunderstandings.

When meeting your Korean counterpart for the first time, always wait to be introduced as third party introductions are generally preferred. Today, it is quite common for Koreans to shake hands with foreign colleagues after a bow, encompassing both cultural styles. To show respect during handshaking, you should ensure that you support your right forearm with the left hand. When departing, a bow is usually sufficient.

Korean business etiquette (Do's and Don'ts):

- DO maintain an element of modesty and humility as these aspects are extremely important in Korean culture. With this in mind, you must try to avoid over-selling previous business achievements.
- DO make direct eye-contact when addressing Korean business professionals, as it is important to indicate your honesty and interest. However, some Koreans do not make eye-contact for any

length of time when in the presence of an authority figure as a sign of respect.

● DO refrain from being overly impatient. The decision making process in Korea is often done collectively and will therefore require more time.

● DON'T address a Korean by his or her given name as it is considered extremely impolite Korean names begin with the family name and are followed by a two-part given name. The correct way to address a Korean is with Mr, Mrs, or Miss together with their family name. You should address your Korean counterparts using appropriate titles until specifically invited to do otherwise.

● DON'T display criticism in public. It should be conducted in private where loss of face will be diminished. In a similar vein, opposing someone directly can also cause a Korean to lose face and should be avoided.

● DON'T use large hand gestures or facial expressions. Talking or laughing loudly is also considered impolite in Korean culture.

≫≫ 4. Business Etiquette in Malaysia

Doing business in Malaysia requires commitment to a long-term effort. Business is often conducted on the basis of personal relationships or rapport.

Business Relationships

Malaysians tend to be reserved in their initial meeting with foreigners and will not generally offer information or enter into in-depth discussions. Compared with Westerners, Malaysians adopt a much more consensual approach in group dynamics. The Western readiness to challenge and probe and to "get right down to business" is not the Malaysian style. Instead, it is appropriate to ask about personal views on issues of general interest to build rapport. Insistence on receiving an "adequate" response to an unanswered question, no matter how important, will only embarrass a Malaysian, especially if other Malaysians are present.

Political issues are highly sensitive and risky, especially since business and politics enjoy closer ties in Malaysia than in many Western countries. Malaysians are proud of their democratic values and institutions. Although the government is embarking on an ambitious privatization program its role in influencing business decisions is still significant. Visitors are not likely to know where particular minefields lie so it is better to confine questions to general politics.

Business Appointments

A prospective Malaysian client must be assured of the commitment of the company and the quality of the product he or she is considering. The best introduction to Malaysia and its business opportunities is through a personal visit since local businesses prefer to meet and deal with their prospective suppliers. When you arrive in Malaysia, you face the challenge of convincing local buyers of your capabilities and the value of your products. The establishment of legitimacy and a long-term commitment is of primary importance to a successful business strategy.

Knowledge of Malaysian business methods and customs is also important. A good local representative will usually arrange meetings, ensure compliance with local business practices and act as a facilitator. Often, the first meeting serves as a get-acquainted session during which the buyer can evaluate your capabilities against current sources. Social interaction can be central to the process of business development.

It is important to plan to arrive on time for business appointments, bearing in mind that traffic can be congested in certain areas at certain times and taxis are not always readily available.

A complete product and company presentation should be made in the initial stages of business contact. This may include literature, specifications, samples, prices, delivery schedule and quality control information to allow the buyer to evaluate both your representatives and the product or service offered. When visiting new markets, experienced exporters ensure that they have produced literature and samples (if appropriate), an ample supply of business cards, company letterhead and thank you notes, extra passport photos and small giveaways with the company name or logo.

Malaysian society is hierarchy-conscious. When meeting with Malaysians, Westerners often make the mistake of addressing the room or group rather than the VIP. Make eye contact. Avoid preaching or lecturing at all costs and listen attentively. Body language such as yawning or lounging during meetings, pointing, and putting feet up on the table is rude and inappropriate, as are loud voices, theatrics, rowdiness and boisterous conversation.

Do not be excessively firm in your handshake. Some Malaysians prefer to touch palms and bring the hand back to the heart to signify a greeting accepted with sincerity. Business cards may be offered with the right hand or both hands. When accepting cards, briefly study a card before putting away. If it is offered to you at a table, it is acceptable to keep the card alongside your plate.

Follow-Up

Thank you notes, samples, brochures and other promised information should be sent as soon as possible. Appropriate follow-up can be crucial to the success of a business visit. Regular correspondence with Malaysian contacts and agents will prove your interest and sincerity. A good local representative will usually arrange meetings, ensure compliance with local business practices and act as a facilitator. Often, the first meeting serves as a get-acquainted session during which the buyer can evaluate your capabilities against current sources. Social interaction can be central to the process of business development.

Dress Code

Malaysia is predominantly a Muslim country and modest dress is advisable. Men should wear a long-sleeved white or plain colored shirt and a tie for business meetings. A jacket can be added when meeting senior officials. A long-sleeved batik shirt and long trousers are often worn for evening events. Shorts and casual shirts should be avoided. Women should dress for business as in Canada, remembering to cover the shoulders and avoid very short skirts and shorts.

Gift-giving Etiquette

When selecting gifts for Muslim Malaysians, avoid products made from pigskin and alcohol, as these goods contravene the laws of Islam. Remember however, that most Chinese Malaysians are not Muslims and would welcome a gift of fine French brandy or Scotch whisky.

Try to avoid using yellow wrapping paper in Malaysia. Yellow is associated with royalty and its use can be interpreted as presumptuous.

Malaysian civil servants must surrender all gifts with a value exceeding RM500 to the national treasury. Under the official government guidelines, civil servants are permitted to buy the goods back if they intend to keep them. Always bear the price of the gift in mind if choosing something for a civil servant.

⫸ 5. Business Etiquette in the Philippines

The Philippine business environment is highly personalized. A proper introduction by a trusted intermediary is the best way to enter this market. The U. S. Commercial Service performs this function for American manufacturers (and their representatives) through our business matchmaking programs, which are described here.

Business Etiquette & Protocol

Business matters are always best dealt with on a face-to-face basis in a warm and pleasant atmosphere. While many Western businesspersons think that time is gold and want to get to the point immediately, the Filipino likes to be indirect, talk about mutual friends and family, exchange pleasantries, and share a joke or two. Only after establishing a cordial atmosphere will people negotiate. No matter what the final result is, the discussions should always end cheerfully. Americans adapting to this cultural practice will have an advantage. To a Filipino, cultivating a friend, establishing a valuable contact and developing personal rapport are what make business wheels turn. The Filipino way of doing business is a confluence of the East and West.

In setting up appointments, especially in government offices, it is most advantageous if a "go-between" or someone with previous connections to that office can make some form of introduction on behalf of the requesting party. Mid-morning or afternoon meetings are preferred, and a follow-up call to confirm the meeting a day before is recommended. Allow for at least fifteen minutes leeway before your Filipino contact arrives for an appointment. For VIPs, waiting time could be longer.

After the requisite small talk following the introductions, a typical business meeting would focus mainly on the agenda at hand. Specific conclusions would not necessarily be achieved during the initial meeting, but Filipinos would usually be amenable to follow up discussions or negotiations. A formal agreement or contract may take a longer time to be finalized compared with what Westerners are used to.

Moreover, as in most Asian cultures, Filipinos would rather avoid "loss of face" or public humiliation. Therefore, Filipino contacts prefer an atmosphere of calm and restraint, avoid direct confrontation, and would typically offer a polite reply coupled with a smile rather than an outright negative feedback to the other party's ideas. A "yes" may mean a lot of things therefore one should be aware of the subtleties of a particular conversation.

Philippine business has its own etiquette. For example, as a show of respect, Filipinos usually address people by their titles (e. g., Architect Cruz, Attorney Jose, Dr. Romero) although the professional might request a more informal approach (e. g., addressing them by their nicknames) after the formal introduction. In dealing with high-ranking government and military officials, it is best to address them by their formal titles (e. g., Secretary Flores, General Alfonso, Director Santos, Admiral Lopez, etc.).

Handing out business cards (preferably bearing your position or title) is standard procedure, although the manners in which the cards are exchanged tend to be rather informal as compared with other cultures. If a Filipino contact gives you a personal number (e. g., home or mobile) aside from what is indicated on the business card, it is usually an invitation to call, and is a good sign for establishing cordial relations.

The foreign businessperson should avoid, as much as possible, personally grappling with the bureaucracy. Customs, for instance, requires many signatures to clear air cargo. The Filipino approach to the problem is to use staff capable of moving through the bureaucracy. Whether getting a driver's license or registering a car, the foreign business executive will benefit by delegating the chore to a someone able to negotiate through a sea of desks, with a smile and a knack for delivering token gifts or keepsakes.

Observing office etiquette is also important. When reprimanding employees, take them aside and do it privately. Be as gentle as possible and always make it a point to end the meeting with some show of personal concern for his family to make him feel he is still part of the team and that the criticism is not personal. Again, this is consistent with avoiding "loss of face".

Filipinos tend to be relaxed in replying to RSVPs. Telephone follow-ups are best, about three days before. Party hosts usually have staff track down guests for a confirmation reply. In a formal occasion, seating is arranged. There is usually a head table for the VIPs. A guest speaker is often the highlight of the dinner. Light entertainment is not unusual. In most instances, important guests accept requests to sing. Americans with vocal talents can score in the Philippines.

Christmas is also a time to show appreciation to people with whom you have regular dealings with, e. g. , the security guard, doorman, messenger, as well as good customers and clients, through token gifts. Gifts could range from baskets of goodies to company giveaways to plain calendars or office items with your company logo.

Office hours for business firms and the Philippine Government normally are from 8 :00 a. m. to 5 :00 p. m. , with a one-hour lunch break. Most banks are open from 9 :00 a. m. to 3 :00 p. m. It is best to attempt to accomplish business objectives in midmorning or late afternoon. Many business deals are completed informally during meals, entertainment, or over a round of golf. Offices are generally closed on Saturdays and Sundays.

Meeting Etiquette

Initial greetings are formal and follow a set protocol of greeting the eldest or most important person first. A handshake, with a welcoming smile, is the standard greeting. Close female friends may hug and kiss when they meet. Use academic, professional, or honorific titles and the person's surname until you are invited to use their first name, or even more frequently, their nickname.

You should offer your business card first. Make sure your business card includes your title. Present and receive business cards with two hands so that it is readable to the recipient. Examine the card briefly before putting it in your business card case. Some senior level executives only give business cards to those of similar rank.

Gift-giving Etiquette

If you are invited to a Filipino home for dinner bring sweets or flowers to the hosts. If you give flowers, avoid chrysanthemums and white lilies. You may send a fruit basket after the event as a thank-you but not before or at the event, as it could be interpreted as meaning you do not think that the host will provide sufficient hospitality. Wrap gifts elegantly as presentation is important. There are no color restrictions as to wrapping paper. Gifts are not opened when received.

Dining Etiquette

Business lunches and dinners are usually arranged personally over the phone and confirmed by the secretary. The person who invites customarily pays. A guest does not order the most expensive items on the menu, unless the host insists otherwise. It is also customary to have a drink before sitting at a dining table. A pleasant atmosphere and a minimum of formality is the tone. Business is not usually discussed until after establishing a convivial ambience, usually after soup or appetizer. If you are invited to a Filipino's house:

● It is best to arrive 15 to 30 minutes later than invited for a large party.

- Never refer to your host's wife as the hostess. This has a different meaning in the Philippines.
- Dress well. Appearances matter and you will be judged on how you dress.
- Compliment the hostess on the house.
- Wait to be asked several times before moving into the dining room or helping yourself to food.
- Wait to be told where to sit. There may be a seating plan.
- Do not start eating until the host invites you to do so.
- Meals are often served family-style or are buffets where you serve yourself.
- A fork and spoon are the typical eating utensils.
- Hold the fork in the left hand and use it to guide food to the spoon in your right hand.
- Whether you should leave some food on your plate or finish everything is a matter of personal preference rather than culture-driven.
- Send a handwritten thank-you note to the hosts in the week following the dinner or party.

Relationship & Communication

Filipinos thrive on interpersonal relationships, so it is advisable to be introduced by a third party. It is crucial to network and build up a cadre of business associates you can call upon for assistance in the future. Business relationships are personal relationships, which mean you may be asked to do favors for colleagues, and they will fully expect you to ask them for favors in return. Once a relationship has been developed it is with you personally, not necessarily with the company you represent. Therefore, if you leave the company, your replacement will need to build their own relationship. Presenting the proper image will facilitate building business relationships. Dress conservatively and well at all times. Filipinos thrive on interpersonal relationships, so it is advisable to be introduced by a third party. It is crucial to network and build up a cadre of business associates you can call upon for assistance in the future.

Business Meeting Etiquette

Appointments are required and should be made 3 to 4 weeks in advance. It is a good idea to reconfirm a few days prior to the meeting, as situations may change. Avoid scheduling meetings the week before Easter. Punctuality is expected. For the most part your Filipino colleagues will be punctual as well. Face-to-face meetings are preferred to other, more impersonal methods such as the telephone, fax, letter or email. Send an agenda and informational materials in advance of the meeting so your colleagues may prepare for the discussion. The actual decision maker may not be at the meeting. Avoid making exaggerated claims. Always accept any offer of food or drink. If you turn down offers of hospitality, your colleagues lose face. It is important to remain for the period of social conversation at the end of the meeting.

Dress Etiquette

Dress is according to venue. Business attire is conservative. Men should wear a dark colored, conservative business suit, at least for the initial meeting. Women should wear a conservative suit, a skirt and blouse, or a dress. Women's clothing may be brightly colored as long as it is of good quality and well tailored. Appearances matter and visitors should dress well.

Summer-weight clothing normally worn in temperate zones is suitable for the Philippines. It is acceptable for businessmen to conduct calls in short or long-sleeved shirt and ties without a coat. Either a two-piece suit or the native "barong tagalog" (a lightweight, long-sleeved shirt worn without a tie) are acceptable, ordinary business attire. Light suits and dresses are appropriate for women.

Business Negotiation

You may never actually meet with the decision maker or it may take several visits to do so.

Decisions are made at the top of the company. Filipinos avoid confrontation if at all possible. It is difficult for them to say "no". Likewise, their "yes" may merely mean "perhaps". At each stage of the negotiation, try to get agreements in writing to avoid confusion or misinterpretation. If you raise your voice or lose your temper, you lose face. Filipinos do business with people more than companies. If you change representatives during negotiations, you may have to start over. Negotiations may be relatively slow. Most processes take a long time because group consensus is necessary. Decisions are often reached on the basis of feelings rather than facts, which is why it is imperative to develop a broad network of personal relationships. Do not remove your suit jacket unless the most important Filipino does.

≫≫ 6. Business Etiquette in Singapore

Business in Singapore is more formal than in many Western countries. There are strict rules of protocol that must be observed. The group (company or department) is viewed as more important than the individual. People observe a strict chain of command, which comes with expectations on both sides. In order to keep others from losing face, much communication will be non-verbal and you must closely watch the facial expressions and body language of people you work with. Personal relationships are the cornerstone of all business relationships.

Building Relationships & Communication

Business is a matter of being tied into the proper network, which is the result of long-standing personal relationships or the proper introductions. Singapore is a group-oriented culture, so links are often based on ethnicity, education or working for the same company. Once you are recognized as part of the group, you will be accepted and expected to obey the unwritten rules of the group and relationships take time to develop. You must be patient as this indicates that your organization is here for the long-term and is not looking only for short-term gains. Always be respectful and courteous when dealing with others as this leads to the harmonious relationships necessary within business. Always be respectful and courteous when dealing with others as this leads to the harmonious relationships necessary within business. Rank is always respected. The eldest person in the group is revered. Rank is always respected. The eldest person in the group is revered. Most Singaporeans are soft-spoken and believe a calm demeanor is superior to a more aggressive style. Watch your body language and facial expressions.

Business Meeting Etiquettes

Business cards are exchanged after the initial introductions. Business cards are exchanged using both hands. If you will be meeting ethnic Chinese, it is a good idea to have one side of your card translated into Mandarin. Have the Chinese characters printed in gold, as this is an auspicious color. Hand your card so the typeface faces the recipient. Examine business cards carefully before putting them in a business card case. Treat business cards with respect. This is indicative of how you will treat the relationship. Your own business cards should be maintained in pristine condition. Remember: never give someone a tattered card.

Appointments are necessary and should be made at least 2 weeks in advance, whenever possible. The most formal way to schedule a meeting is to write to the person concerned, although most Singaporeans will schedule an appointment by telephone, fax, or e-mail. Do not try to schedule meetings during Chinese New Year (late January/early February), since many businesses close for the entire week. You should arrive at meetings on time. Punctuality is a virtue. There will be period of small talk before getting down to business discussions.

Since questioning authority is a taboo, it is important to encourage questions when after making a presentation and then smile when a question is eventually asked. Presentations should be accompanied by backup material, including charts and figures. Never disagree or criticize someone who is senior to you in rank as it will cause both of you to lose face and may destroy the business relationship. Pay attention to non-verbal communication.

Business Negotiation

Businessmen always send a list of people who will be attending the negotiations and their title well in advance and wait to be told where to sit. There is a strict hierarchy that must be followed. Business negotiations happen at a slow pace.

Singaporeans are non-confrontational. They will not overtly say "no"; likewise, their "yes" does not always signify agreement. They give a respectful pause of up to 15 seconds before answering a question. You should not start speaking too quickly or you will miss the answer.

You should be prepared with a mental list of concessions, you would be willing to make that would not injure your own business. Singaporeans are tough negotiators on price and deadlines.

Decisions are consensus driven. Avoid losing your temper or you will lose face and damage your relationship. If you are signing a contract with ethnic Chinese, the signing date may be determined by an astrologer or a geomancer (feng shui man).

➤➤ 7. Business Etiquette in Thailand

Thai value systems regarding dress, social behavior, religion, authority figures, and sexuality are much more conservative than those of the average Westerner. Although the Thais are an extremely tolerant and forgiving race of people blessed with a gentle religion and an easygoing approach to life, visitors would do well to observe proper social customs to avoid embarrassment and misunderstanding.

Thai people are extremely polite and their behavior is tightly controlled by etiquette, much of it based on their Buddhist religion. It is, if nothing else, an extremely non-confrontational society, in which public dispute or criticism is to be avoided at all costs. To show anger or impatience or to raise your voice is a sign of weakness and lack of mental control. It is also counter productive, since the Thai who will smile, embarrassed by your outburst of anger or frustration is far less likely to be helpful than if you had kept better control of your emotions.

The head is the most sacred part of the body, so should not be touched. The feet are the least sacred, so when sitting they should not point at anyone — most Thais sit on the floor with their feet tucked under their bodies behind them. To point, particularly with one's foot, is extremely insulting.

Avoid touching Thai people, it is too intimate a gesture and an invasion of personal space.

When eating, it is considered very rude to blow your nose or to lick you fingers. The right hand must be used to pick up food that is eaten with the fingers.

Business Attire

Thailand is a very hot, tropical country, so allowances are made in terms of clothing. However, as in most Asian countries, a person is often judged on their appearance and it always pays to dress well. A suit is preferred for formal meetings but a business shirt and tie for men, or dress or skirt and blouse for women, is appropriate for less formal situations.

Revealing clothing, worn by either men or women, is a little disgusting to most Thais. Short shorts, low-cut dresses and T-shirts and skimpy (or no) bathing suits come into this category. In temples, long trousers or skirts must be worn, and monks should on no account be touched in any way by women (or men for that matter). Shoes should always be removed when entering temples and private houses. For this reason, most Thais wear slip-on shoes to avoid constantly tying and untying laces.

Clothing from the lower parts of the body should never be left anywhere in a high position.

This applies particularly to socks and underwear, but also to shorts and skirts. This is the case even when washing and drying clothes. Thais have two clothes lines — a high one for most clothes and a low one for underwear and socks. Some laundries will not accept underwear for cleaning — they would be impressed with your asking if this is the case.

Greeting and Meeting

Address a Thai man or woman by their first name, not their surname, using the prefix "*Khun*" instead of Mr. or Mrs. For example, former Thai Prime Minister Chuan Leekpai should be referred Address a Thai man or woman by their first name, not their surname, using the prefix "*Khun*" as Khun Chuan. It is not considered informal or familiar to call Thais by their first name.

Thais normally greet Westerners with a handshake in business situations, however the traditional Thai greeting is a *wai* — a gesture where the hands are placed together at chest height and the head is bowed slightly.

As in all Asian countries, business cards are useful when introducing yourself for the first time. Thais do not traditionally shake hands; the *wai* is the usual greeting. The hands are placed together as in prayer, and raised upwards towards the face, while the head is lowered in a slight bow. The height to which the hands should be raised depends on the status of the person you are *waiing*. In the case of monks, dignitaries and old people the hands are raised to the bridge of the nose; with equals only as far as the chest. Young people and inferiors are not *waied*, but nodded slightly to. You will be regarded as a little foolish should you *wai* to them, or go about *waiing* everyone, putting them on the spot and making yourself appear foolish.

When you consider that shaking hands, and kissing, are perhaps the easiest means of passing germs, the *wai* is in fact a suitable greeting.

It is very easy, when entering a foreign culture for the first time, to make mistakes in etiquette. If you do so, just smile, politely *wai* the person you may have offended, and all is usually forgiven.

Gifts

They do not buy gifts which come in a set of six, as this number is considered inauspicious in Thailand. Red is the best color for wrapping paper in Thailand, as it is associated with wealth and prosperity. Gifts of footwear may be considered inappropriate in Thailand, because the foot is considered the least sacred part of the human body.

Business Communication

Although Thai people appreciate punctuality when conducting business, deadlines are often overlooked and it is necessary to allow for this when scheduling meetings.

Never contradict or criticize anybody in public. Thais, like Chinese people, have a refined sense of public image and it is easy to cause someone to "lose face". To complain that a Thai is late for an appointment may cause them to lose face and thereby disrupt the course of business Never joke about the monarchy. Thai people treat their monarchy with great reverence and the Royal family should never be insulted or criticised.

Buddhism is Thailand's national religion and priests must always receive a high level of respect. Women should never touch a monk or his robe. When handing an object to a monk, a woman should use an intermediary or place the object in a position where it can be retrieved by the monk.

Thai people regard the head as the most precious part of the body. Never touch a person (including children) on the head, or anywhere above the shoulders. In the same way, Thais regard the feet as the least sacred part of the body and it is considered offensive to point with the feet or even show the sole of the shoe or foot to another person. It is therefore necessary to take care when crossing your legs.

Business Etiquette in America

≫ 1. Business Etiquettes in Latin America

Latin America stretches from the Texas border to the tip of Tierra del Fuego. Latin America is predominantly Catholic among its Spanish and Portuguese speaking populations and primarily non-Catholic among its native inhabitants. The culture is predominantly patriarchal in nature. Rigid divisions between work and home exist: Men are in business and women are at home with the family. Anyone going to Nicaragua, Guatemala, El Salvador, Colombia, Chile, or Peru should know enough about the current political climate to avoid discussions that might skewer business dealings.

Handshakes

Handshakes are firm and relatively brief. Constant eye contact during a handshake is crucial in Mexico and Argentina. Men shake hands with man and women shake hands with women in some countries. In Brazil, Peru, and Mexico, men and women also shake hands, with the woman countries. In Brazil, Peru, and Mexico, men and women also shake hands, with the woman extending her hand first.

Male friends hug each other upon seeing each other. Female friends kiss each other on the cheek and touch each other's arms. And throughout Latin America, expect your conversational partner to stand close to you and look you in the eyes. Don't move back and don't waver in your eye contact.

Names and Titles

When you meet for the first time use your last name and whatever titles you have. Latin American surnames are composed of both the paternal name, which comes first, and the maternal name.

Business Attire

You won't go wrong by dressing conservatively: suits and ties for men, unrevealing business suits and long dresses for women. Argentina is probably the moat formal of the Latin American countries and Brazil the least formal. Venezuelans enjoy expensive accessories, as long as they're good taste.

Dinning and Entertaining

Business lunches are common throughout Latin America, and usually long, from 1:00 or 2:00 p. m. until 3:00 or 4:00 p. m. Dinner is a purely social event, and can occur very late; it's not unusual to sit down to dinner at 10:00 p. m. or 11:00 p. m. throughout Latin America. In general, you should keep your hands above the table at all times while eating, and pass food and drink with your right hand.

Gift-giving Etiquette

You may be a few minutes late for dinner across the region, but you should never be early. Small host gifts are accepted in most Latin countries. Venezuelans do not entertain at home very much. It's an unusual honor to be invited, so make the host gift something special.

Social Taboos

If you do business with Latin Americans, be aware that the following gestures can cause problems:
- The sign for "OK" formed by your forefinger and thumb is offensive in Brazil.
- Putting your hands on your hips is a gesture signaling a challenge in Argentina, and putting your feet on the table is rude.
- Raising your fist to head level is a gesture associated with Communism in Chile.
- Putting your hands in your pockets is rude in Mexico.

≫ 2. Business Etiquettes in Brazil

In Brazil, people need to know who they are doing business with before they can work effectively. Brazilians prefer face-to-face meetings to written communication as it allows them to know the person with whom they are doing business. The individual they deal with is more important than the company. Since this is a group culture, it is important that you do not do anything to embarrass a Brazilian. Criticizing an individual causes that person to lose face with the others in the meeting. The person making the criticism also loses face, as they have disobeyed the unwritten rule. Communication is often informal and does not rely on strict rules of protocol.

Anyone who feels they have something to say will generally add their opinion. It is considered acceptable to interrupt someone who is speaking. Face-to-face, oral communication is preferred over written communication. At the same time, when it comes to business agreements, Brazilians insist on drawing up detailed legal contracts.

Meeting Etiquettes

Men shake hands when greeting one another, while maintaining steady eye contact. Women generally kiss each other, starting with the left and alternating cheeks. Hugging and backslapping are common greetings among Brazilian friends. If a woman wishes to shake hands with a man, she should extend her hand first.

Business cards are exchanged during introductions with everyone at a meeting. It is advisable, although not required, to have the other side of your business card translated into Portuguese and present your business card with the Portuguese side facing the recipient.

Business appointments are required and can often be scheduled on short notice; however, it is best to make them 2 to 3 weeks in advance and confirm the meeting in writing. It is not uncommon for appointments to be cancelled or changed at the last minute. In Sao Paulo and Brasilia it is important to arrive on time for meetings. In Rio de Janeiro and other cities it is acceptable to arrive a few minutes late for a meeting.

You should be patient if you are kept waiting. Brazilians see time as something outside their control and the demands of relationships takes precedence over adhering to a strict schedule. Meetings are generally rather informal. You are expected to be interrupted while you are speaking or making a presentation. You should not appear frustrated with your Brazilian counterparts and try to avoid confrontations.

Gift-giving Etiquette

If you are invited to a Brazilian's house, bring the hostess flowers or a small gift. Orchids are considered a very nice gift, but avoid purple ones. Avoid giving anything purple or black as these are mourning colors. Handkerchiefs are also associated with funerals, so they do not make good gifts. Gifts are opened when received.

Dining Etiquette

If you are invited to a Brazilian's house, please remember:
● Arrive at least 30 minutes late if the invitation is for dinner.
● Arrive up to an hour late for a party or large gathering.
● Brazilians dress with a flair and judge others on their appearance. Casual dress is more formal than in many other countries. Always dress elegantly and err on the side of over-dressing rather than under-dressing.
● If you did not bring a gift to the hostess, flowers the next day are always appreciated.

Dress Etiquette

Brazilians pride themselves on dressing well. Men should wear conservative, dark colored business suits. Three-piece suits typically indicate that someone is an executive. To feel comfortable in Brazil's sweltering, tropical climate, wear clothing made of light materials and colors that will help keep you cool. Light cottons and similar natural fibers are usually reliable choices. Women should wear suits or dresses that are elegant and feminine with good quality accessories. Manicures are expected.

Appearance is vital in any business culture, however in Brazil the subtle differences are more acceptable; for instance you may wear jeans and a nice shirt and blazer to a meeting and be totally accepted. In Brazil there is a lot more fashion trends in business attire than in other courtiers.

If you are wearing a three-piece suit in winter it is fashionable, but not in summer. Most Brazilian suits, unlike those made in the US, are tailor-made and that is what distinguishes your position. One distinguishing factor is if the materials in your suit are local or imported.

Men should wear dark suits in black, charcoal gray, or navy blue. Again depending on the industry, light colors in the summer months are acceptable. Dark is better if you are traveling because it hides any dirt better.

They usually select ties that are well-made and conservative. There is easy access to imported silk ties, but they are not conservative. They can be very flashy.

Ensure that your shoes are polished and kept in excellent condition. Or if you want to — depending on the industry — you can wear sandals or tennis shoes.

Wardrobe options for women include conservative dresses, suits, pantsuits, skirts, and blouses. While you should dress conservatively, strive for an elegant, rather than "frumpish", appearance.

Women's nails should be well cared for. Makeup is not a strong feature among Brazilian women, who lean towards the natural look. Women's nails should be well cared for. Makeup is not a strong feature among Brazilian women, who lean towards the natural look.

Business Negotiation

You can expect questions about your company since Brazilians are more comfortable doing business with people and companies they know and wait for your Brazilian colleagues to raise the business subject. Never rush the relationship — building time. Brazilians take time when negotiating. Do not rush them or appear impatient. Brazilians take time when negotiating. You can expect a great deal of time to be spent reviewing details. Often the people you negotiate with will not have decision-making authority. It is advisable to hire a translator if your Portuguese is not fluent. Use local lawyers and accountants for negotiations. Brazilians resent an outside legal presence. Brazilian business is hierarchical. Decisions are made by the highest-ranking person.

Brazilians negotiate with people not companies. Do not change your negotiating team or you may have to start over from the beginning.

⋙ 3. Business Etiquettes in Colombia

Colombians are termed as "indirect communicators" — this means there is more information within body language and context rather than the words, i. e. , if you ask someone to do something and they reply "I will have to see", it would be up to you to read between the lines and realize that they can not do it.

The reason for this way of communicating is to protect relationships and face. This means people that are used to speaking directly and openly must tame their communication style as it could cause offense. Although they can be indirect, Colombians can also become very animated. This should not be mistaken for aggression. Avoid confrontation at all cost. If someone has made a mistake, do not expose it publicly as this will lead to a loss of face and a ruined relationship.

Meeting and Greeting

Relationship building is crucial — it may be a good idea to invest time in establishing trust for the first few meetings. Time is not an issue in meetings — they will last as long as they need to last. Do not try and rush proceedings. Although there may be an agenda, meetings do not always follow a linear path. An agenda will serve as a starting point and after that issues are addressed as an when.

Men shake hands with direct eye contact. While shaking hands, they use the appropriate greeting for the time of day: "buenos dias" (good day), "buenas tardes" (good afternoon), or "buenas noches" (good evening/night). Women often grasp forearms rather than shaking hands. Once a friendship has developed, greetings become warmer and a lot more hands on — men will embrace and pat each other on the shoulder (known as an "abrazo") and women kiss once on the right cheek.

Most Colombians have both a maternal and paternal surname and will use both. The father's surname is listed first and is the one used in conversation.

It is a good idea to try and have one side of your business card translated into Spanish.

Gift-giving Etiquette

Gifts are given for birthdays and Christmas or the Epiphany (January 6th). In Colombia a girl's 15th birthday is considered an important milestone. Gifts are given for birthdays and Christmas or the Epiphany (January 6th). Here are some handy tips:

● When going to a Colombian's home, bring fruit, a potted plant, or quality chocolates for the hostess.

● Flowers should be sent in advance.

● Do not give lilies or marigolds as they are used at funerals. Roses are liked.
● If you are going to a girl's 15th birthday, gold is the usual gift.
● Imported alcohol (especially spirits) is very expensive and make excellent gifts.
● Wrapped gifts are not opened when received.

Dining Etiquette

Dining etiquette is quite formal in Colombia as they tend to give importance to decorum and presentation. Below are some basic tips — if you are ever unsure the general rule is "observe and follow":

● Wait to be seated by the host.
● Hands should be kept visible when eating.
● Do not rest elbows on the table.
● The host will say "buen provecho" (enjoy or have a good meal) as an invitation to start eating.
● It is polite to try everything you are given.
● Unusually all food is eaten with utensils — even fruit is cut into pieces with a knife and fork.
● It is considered polite to leave a small amount of food on your plate when you have finished eating.
● It is courteous to shake hands both upon meeting and departing.
● Men should wait for a woman to extend her hand.
● Greetings should take some time — ensure you engage in some small talk, i. e. , ask about family, health and business.
● Eye contact is viewed positively.
● Wait for the other party to initiate a change to first names.
● Do not use a toothpick at the table.

≫ 4. Business Etiquettes in the United States

This culture stresses individual initiative and achievement. Moreover, Americans can also be competitive in both work and leisure. The concept "time is money" is taken seriously in U. S. business culture. Businesspeople are used to making up their minds quickly and decisively. They value information that is straightforward and to the point.

American businesspeople are opportunistic and willing to take chances. Opportunism and risk taking often result in Americans going for the biggest possible slice of the business, 100% if possible. They tend to dislike periods of silence during negotiations and in conversations, in general. They may continue to speak simply to avoid silence.

In general, Americans will not hesitate to answer "no". Businesspeople are direct and will not hesitate to disagree with you. This communication style often causes embarrassment to business travelers who are unaccustomed to dealing with Americans or direct communication in general.

Persistence is another characteristic you will frequently encounter in American businesspeople; there is a prevailing belief that there is always a solution. Moreover, they will explore all options when negotiations are at an impasse. Consistency is common among American businesspeople: when they agree to a deal, they rarely change their minds.

In the United States, little business is conducted on Sundays. This is the standard day of worship for many religions. If your stay in the U.S. is short, however, your American business counterparts may arrange to do business on this day.

Business Dress

Business suit and tie are appropriate in all major cities. Wear dark colored business suits in classic colors of gray and navy. For an important formal meeting, choose a white dress shirt, for less formal a light blue shirt will still give you a conservative appearance.

Women should wear a suit or dress with jacket in major cities. Wearing classic clothing and classic colors of navy, gray, ivory, and white will ensure you give a confident and conservative appearance.

Rural areas and areas with extremely warm summers have more informal wardrobe requirements. Women may wear a business dress, or skirt and blouse, in rural areas.

For a first meeting, you cannot go wrong if you dress conservatively. Afterwards, you may want to follow the example of your American counterparts.

In U.S. business culture, dress tends to vary. In some parts of the country — the east in particular — most people wear business suits. In other areas, such as the west coast, a more relaxed approach to dressing is the norm in many workplaces. Executives in most regions of the country, however, usually dress quite formally

Business suits or dresses are often the standard attire for women. Pantsuits, in classic styles, are also acceptable. Accessorizing, which adds flair to even very simple outfits, is also practiced here. When not working, feel free to dress casually. In their leisure hours, you will notice that Americans wear a wide range of casual items, such as running shoes, T-shirts, jeans, shorts, baseball caps, etc.

Communications

Business conversation *may* take place during meals. However, many times you will find more social conversation taking place during the actual meal.

Business meetings may be arranged as breakfast meetings, luncheon meetings, or dinner meetings depending on time schedules and necessity. Generally a dinner, even though for business purposes, is treated as a social meal and a time to build rapport.

Americans often offer a firm handshake, lasting 3-5 seconds, upon greeting and leaving. Maintain good eye contact during your handshake. If you are meeting several people at once, maintain eye contact with the person you are shaking hands with, until you are moving on the next person.

Good eye contact during business and social conversations shows interest, sincerity and confidence. Good friends may briefly embrace, although the larger the city, usually the more formal the behavior. Introductions include one's title if appropriate, or Mr. , Ms, Mrs. and the full name. Business cards are generally exchanged during introductions. However, they may be exchanged when one party is leaving.

A smile is a sign of friendliness, and in rural areas you may be greeted with a "hello" rather than a handshake. Ask permission to smoke before lighting a cigarette or cigar. Due to health concerns, you may or may not be given permission.

Gift-giving Etiquette

Business gifts are often presented after the deal is closed. In most situations, gifts are usually unwrapped immediately and shown to all assembled. In many cases, the best gifts are those that come from your country. You may not receive a gift in return right away

During the Holiday season (late November through the first week of January) , gifts are exchanged. For your business associates, you can give gifts such as useful items for the office, liquor or wine. Choose gifts with no religious connotations (i. e. don't buy Christmas ornaments) , unless you are certain of the religious background of your associates. While Christmas is the dominant celebration, and is widely commercialized during this period, people may be celebrating many other holidays during this period (i. e. Hanukkah, Kwanzaa) .

When you visit a home, it is not necessary to take a gift, although it is always appreciated. Flowers, a potted plant, or a bottle of wine are good gift choices. If you wish to give flowers, you can have them sent in advance to relieve your host or hostess from taking care of them when you arrive.

If you stay in a U. S. home for a few days, a gift is appropriate. You may also write a thank-you note. Taking someone out for a meal or other entertainment is another popular gift. Gifts for women such as perfume or clothing are usually inappropriate. They are considered too personal. Gifts for children are often a thoughtful and appreciated gesture, but take into account the values of the parents. Many parents would object to your giving a toy gun or a violent video game to their child.

Business Negotiation

In a meeting, the participants will proceed with business usually after some brief, preliminary "small talk" about topics unrelated to the business at hand. This is generally practiced to ease tensions and create a comfortable environment before entering into business matters. Topics may range from sports, weather, or other smaller business topics. Personal matters should not be discussed during this time, or any time in the negotiation. Usually, business is conducted at an extremely fast pace.

Regardless of the negotiator, company policy is always followed. Though they are risk-takers, American businesspeople will also have a financial plan which must be followed. Americans regard negotiating as problem-solving through "give and take" based on respective strengths. Therefore, they will often emphasize their financial strength and/or position of power.

In negotiations, points are made by the accumulation of objective facts. This evidence is sometimes biased by faith in the ideologies of democracy, capitalism, and consumerism. The subjective feelings of the participants are not as much of a factor. Therefore, they will not spend much time seeking consensus.

Often, American businesspeople try to extract an oral agreement at the first meeting. However, U. S. salespeople sometimes bring final contracts to first meetings with prospective clients. In large firms, contracts under $ 10,000 can often be approved by one middle manager in a single meeting.

Business Cards

Your business card will not be refused, but you may not always receive one in return. Try not to be offended — in the U. S. , the rituals involved in exchanging business cards are sometimes not observed as closely as in other cultures.

The recipient of your card will probably place it into a wallet, which a man may put in the back pocket of his pants. This gesture is done for convenience and is not meant to be a sign of disrespect, as it might be in other cultures.

In many cases, business cards are not exchanged unless you want to contact the person later.

Dining and Entertaining

Dinner is the main meal of the day and can start between 5:30 and 8:00 p. m. If you are invited out for a business meal, the host will usually pay. If your host does not offer to pay, you should be prepared to pay for your own meal.

When eating out, the cost is sometimes shared with friends or colleagues. "Getting separate checks" and "going Dutch" refer to paying for your own portion of the bill. It is also common to "split the bill," where the cost of the meal is shared equally among the individuals.

If you invite a U. S. counterpart out socially, you should make it clear whether you wish to pay. Common ways to express this wish include "It's on me" or "I'd like to buy you lunch".

There are a variety of ways to beckon a server. For example, you can make eye contact and raise your eyebrows, briefly wave to get his or her attention, or mouth the word for what you want such as "water" or "coffee". To call for the check, you can make a writing gesture or mouth the word "check, please". You can also get a server's attention by saying, "Excuse me," as they walk by. Americans use "Please" and "Thank you" frequently in dining situations; politeness is valued.

It is common to invite a business guest to one's home in the U. S. This is considered a gesture to show goodwill between associates. Be aware that it is a custom in many U. S. homes to give guests a tour of the general rooms of the house when guests arrive.

If you will be entertained in a home, expect the host's or hostesses's spouse or partner to be a full participant in the conversation. Unlike some other cultures, it's perfectly acceptable to refuse an offer of food or drink. In most cases, the host probably won't urge you to eat. Don't be afraid to ask for something. Use manners and ask politely.

Business Meetings

A handshake is the customary greeting for both men and women. Americans tend to refrain from greetings that involve hugging and other close physical contact, except with family members and friends. For the most part, they are unreceptive to being touched during conversation and other social situations. The standard space between you and your conversation partner should be about two feet. Most U. S. executives will be uncomfortable standing at a closer distance.

Business meetings are also frequently held over lunch, which begins at 12:00 noon and sometimes lasts until 2:00 p. m. Lunch is usually a lighter meal, since work continues directly afterward. Be careful about alcoholic beverages such as wine or beer at lunch. You may find some companies where this is common, and others that have strict policies against alcoholic drinks during lunch hours. Follow the lead of your host and order a soft drink if you are unsure.

To show approval, there are two common gestures: the "O. K." sign, formed by making a circle of the thumb and index finger, and the "Thumbs Up" sign, formed by making a fist and pointing the thumb upward.

Direct eye contact conveys that you are sincere, although it should not be too intense. Certain ethnic groups may look away to show respect.

When sitting, U. S. citizens often look very relaxed. They may sometimes sit with the ankle of one leg on their knee or prop their feet up on chairs or desks. In formal business situations, however, you're advised to maintain good posture and a less casual pose. Crossing legs knee over knee is not considered arrogant, as in other cultures. In the U. S. this position is common and considered professional.

≫ 5. Business Etiquette in Canada

Canada has a population just less than 30 million people in a country twice the area of the United States. The heritage of Canada was French and English; however, significant immigration from Asia and Europe's non-French and English countries has broadened Canada's cultural richness. The majority of Canadians have individualism ranked highest. Success is measured by personal achievement. Canadians tend to be self-confident and open to discussions on general topics; however, they hold their personal privacy off limits to all but the closest friends.

Dress Etiquette

Men should wear a dark conservative business suit with tie, especially in cities. Build a wardrobe based on classic lines (selecting suits with a traditional lapel width, and ties staying within a traditional width range). Conservative colors of navy and gray, and shirts in white and light blue.

Women should wear a conservative business suit or dress, especially in cities. Select your clothing with classic lines and colors in mind. Navy, gray, ivory, and white are the basics to work with. The major cities can be very sophisticated.

New or trendy clothing is a poor choice. Older, classic clothing that is clean and neat is more valued. Choosing quality, natural fibers for your wardrobe will give you this look. Quality leather shoes are important to completing this look.

Rural areas are less formal, but stay conservative in your wardrobe. Even with cold winter weather you may find yourself in a skirt or dress. Add a good quality long coat with minimal and classic detail to your wardrobe. In addition to navy and gray, a classic camel coat, or a lined Burberry may be a good addition. This will work for a sophisticated city meeting, or a more casual rural meeting.

Casual attire is appropriate when you are not working. The weather and activity will dictate what you will be wearing. Build a casual wardrobe using the classic colors (camel is additional color for casual). You will look professional, even though relaxed.

Behavior

Be punctual for meetings and appointments, as promptness is valued. In French areas, time is more relaxed. However, you will be expected to arrive at the appointed time, even if the French attending the meeting don't.

Always maintain a reserved demeanor, and follow good rules of etiquette. Traditions and gracious manners are part of the culture, even in more rural areas. If you travel to different cities or areas, pay attention to local customs. By being observant, you will respect the pace and nuances of each area.

Do not eat while walking in public. Plan your time so you can stop in a café or restaurant to enjoy your snack.

Gift-giving Etiquette

Gifts are not routinely given. If you do give a gift when you arrive or when you are leaving, make it a modest one. A lavish gift, though accepted, would be frowned upon.

Gifts *are* given to celebrate finalizing a negotiation, a contract, or a project. Gifts for the office, a nice bottle of wine or liquor would be appropriate.

Dinning and Entertaining

Taking a business associate to nice meal or an evening sporting event, play, or symphony is always a nice gesture.

Invitations to private homes are rare. Occasionally, in the western provinces, you may be invited to someone's home. If you are invited, you may take candy, flowers, or liquor to the host or hostess.

Wait for your host to start a business conversation during or following a meal. Traditionally, business is not discussed during dinner; however, this is slowly changing.

Personal space and body movement or gestures differ between the English and the French provinces and cities. In English areas, body movement is minimal, there is rarely touching other than handshakes, and personal space — how close someone stands — is about two feet. In French areas, people stand closer together, people will frequently touch, and gestures are more expressive.

Communications

Use a firm handshake with good eye contact when meeting and leaving. Both French and English areas use and expect a firm handshake.

French Canadians will shake hands more frequently, even with a subsequent encounter the same day. Others may just nod or smile at a subsequent encounter on the same day.

Men will wait for a woman to extend her hand for a handshake. Use a person's title if he or she has one. Otherwise, use Mr. , Mrs. , Miss and the surname.

English is spoken in most of Canada. French is spoken in Quebec, and some area of Nova Scotia Brunswick

French Canadians may use their first name when talking to you on the telephone, but will generally use their full name when meeting you in person.

Be open and friendly in your conversation. If you are naturally reserved in your behavior, you will appear confident and credible. If your natural tendency is large sweeping arm gestures, restrain yourself when meeting and talking with Canadians — other than with French Canadians.

French Canadians stand closer and are more demonstrative when talking. For French Canadians, print all material in French and English. Don't be boastful, and don't overstate your product or service's capabilities. You could implicate your company in a legal situation.

If you are from the U. S. , don't say, "we Americans", inferring you are including your Canadian hosts or guests in your reference. Canada is a distinct country with its own wonderful history and culture.

The "V for Victory" sign is an insult if your palm is facing yourself. If you must use this sign, face your palm outward.

Business Etiquette in Africa

» 1. Business Etiquette in Africa

The northern countries bordering the Mediterranean are Islamic, and you can expect that the kind of lavish generosity, indirect business discussions, expansive sense of time, and second class citizen status for women found in the Arabic countries is found here too.

Names and Titles

You can never go wrong by using last names and titles when you first meet. Academic titles add a great deal of luster.

Business Attire

Conservative is the keyword. In particular hot countries, some easing up on the dark business suit is permitted. And, of course, your host will not be bound to Western dress. He may show up in dressy traditional attire.

Dining and Entertaining

Africans are justly famous for the pleasure they take in eating and entertaining and for their generosity. If you are invited to someone's home almost anywhere in Africa, be prepared — your host will go all out to impress you. In many countries, you will find no utensils of any kind and will be expected to eat with your hands. Remember, in Muslim countries, not to eat with your left hands. Watch your hosts in other countries for similar taboos. When in doubt, do as your host does.

Gifts

In Jewish homes, a gift of flowers to the host is preferred. but gifts to the host are frowned on in Muslim homes. and under no circumstances, should you give a Muslim a gift of alcohol, a picture of anyone or of any animal or anything made from pigs.

Social Taboos

In most of the Middle East, it's bad manners for an outsider to discuss politics or religion. Showing the soles of your shoes or feet is rude in Turkey and in the Arabic countries, as is openly disagreeing with someone. And in Turkey, fist names are only used when you know the person very well. The thumbs-up sign is rude in Muslim countries.

≫ 2. Business Etiquette in South Africa

South African table manners can greatly vary, depending on who you are with. If you are dining with a South African of European descent, they might cut a burger up with a fork and knife. If dining with a South African of Indian descent, they might eat a rice dish with their hands.

One important thought to keep in mind during your travels to South Africa is to remain adaptable. South Africa is a melting pot, with people of African, European, and Indian backgrounds, and it is reflected in their culture. Below is a list of South African etiquette tips, but when in doubt, follow the lead of those around you.

Dressing Etiquette

Business attire is becoming more informal in many companies. However, for the first meeting, it is best to dress more conservatively. Men should wear dark colored conservative business suits. Remember:

- DO wear what you normally would wear when in urban parts, but dress nicely. In South African urban cultures, people usually wear typical Western attire.
- DON'T wear sneakers or shorts unless it's a casual affair, such as a barbecue, taking a walk, or going to the beach.
- DO wear a suit for formal business meetings, and for less formal meetings men should wear a sports coat without a tie, and women should wear smart, yet casual clothes.

Dining Etiquette

If you are invited to a South African's house:

- Arrive on time if invited to dinner.
- Contact the hostess ahead of time to see if she would like you to bring a dish.
- Wear casual clothes. This may include jeans or pressed shorts.

It is a good idea to check with the hosts in advance. In Johannesburg, casual is dressier than in other parts of the country. Do not wear jeans or shorts unless you have spoken to the hosts.

Offer to help the hostess with the preparation or clearing up after a meal is served. Offer to help the hostess with the preparation or clearing up after a meal is served.

When eating, remember:

- DON'T cut bread rolls. Instead, break them into small bite-sized pieces on a side plate.
- DON'T leave food on your plate when you're done eating.
- DOcross your knife and fork on your plate to indicate that you are still eating.
- DO place your knife and fork closely together next to your plate to indicate that you are done eating.
- DO put your napkin on your lap upon being seated.
- DO be adaptable with your table manners. Because South Africa is such a diverse country, table manners can vary depending on your dining partners.

Tipping

- DO tip 10%-20% at a restaurant, but do check the bill to ensure that the tip hasn't been included already.
- DO tip tour guides and bus drivers at the end of the day. Usually it is R10.00 per person on a day tour. The guide and driver will split it.
- DO pay hotel porters R3.00 a bag.

Gift-giving and Accepting Gifts

- DO open your gift immediately.
- DO use either both hands and your right hand to give or receive a present. Don't use your left.
- DON'T spend more than fifty U.S. dollars.
- DO give gifts such as cigars, whiskey, wine, a souvenir from your hometown, or flowers. There are no taboos in terms of giving flowers, although carnations are sometimes associated with funerals.
- DO send a thank-you note. Either a handwritten note or an email will do.

Body Language and Gestures

- DON'T touch someone's arm or stand too close to someone.
- DO keep your hands and arms at your sides when standing or keep them loosely folded on your lap when sitting.
- DON'T put your hands in your pockets, on your hips, or cross your arms in front of you.
- DON'T yawn without covering your mouth, bite your nails, spit, chew with your mouth. Open, audibly sniffle, or pick your nose.

Greeting

- DO shake hands upon meeting someone.

● DO expect women to greet each other with a kiss on the cheek.

Visiting Someone's Home

● DO bring wine or flowers when visiting someone's home.
● DON'T remove your shoes unless entering a Muslim home.
● DO expect a meal at a white South African's home to be a poolside barbecue.

Business

● DO give a gift to your business associates.
● DO use titles and last names when talking to associates.
● DON'T rush negotiations.
● DO schedule meetings two weeks in advance.
● DON'T use slang or bad language in a business meeting.
● DONT be late! In fact, try to arrive to an appointment five minutes early. South Africans are punctual and being late is considered rude.

Conversation

● DO be aware of South Africa's racial terminology. Black is the preferred term for those of African ancestry and white is for those of Caucasian ancestry who speak English or Afrikaans.
● DON'T call Afrikaners "Dutchmen" and don't call Afrikaans "Kitchen Dutch". Afrikaners don't consider themselves.

Safari Etiquette

● DON'T imitate animal sounds, throw objects, or corner a wild animal. You never know how an animal will react, and it could be dangerous.
● DO listen to the guide. Respect their judgment; they're the expert!
● DON'T smoke while on a safari.
● DON'T litter. It's disrespectful and can be dangerous to animals. If you bring something in, take it out with you.
● DON'T take anything you find while on a safari.
● DON'T feed animals. DO tip the rangers $ 10 per guest each day. In a private vehicle, pay $ 20 per guest each day. Gifts are also nice in addition to a tip.
● DO tip other safari staff members (such as valets, butlers, waiters, cleaners) $ 5 per guest each day.

Because South Africa is such a diverse country, you will find that there are a variety of customs. Keep the above etiquette in mind and enjoy your trip to South Africa.

⋙ 3. Business Etiquette in Nigeria

Did you know that in Nigeria, you traditionally eat with your hands? You should try it out on your trip to Nigeria! You will be given finger bowls and towels to keep clean. Don't ever eat with your left hand, though. The left hand is considered unclean. If you're uncomfortable eating with your hands, it's OK to ask for utensils.

While in Nigeria, you will find that Nigerians are warm, polite, and caring. As a guest to their country, you should practice the same courtesy and respect by learning a bit about their culture and etiquette. Below is a list of etiquette to take with you on your trip to Nigeria.

Dressing Etiquette

● DON'T wear revealing clothes, if you are a woman.
● DO wear suits for business functions.
● DON'T wear shorts at business meetings or restaurants, but they are fine for the beach or casual social gatherings.

Food Drinks

● DO try eating with your hands! You'll be given finger bowls and towels. It's OK to ask for utensils if you're uncomfortable eating with your hands.
● DON'T use your left hand at all. Don't eat with it, pass food with it, or receive food with it.

Gift-giving Etiquette

If you are invited to a South African's home, bring flowers, good quality chocolates, or a bottle of good South African wine to the hostess. Remember:
● DO wrap presents. Any color wrapping paper is fine.
● DO say that a gift came from a female relative, if you're a man giving a gift. Say it came from your wife, sister, mother, etc.
● DO bring gifts for children.
● DO bring gifts such as fruit, nuts, or chocolate if invited to a Nigerian's home for a meal.

Greeting Etiquette

There are several greeting styles in South Africa depending upon the ethnic heritage of the person you are meeting. When dealing with foreigners, most South Africans shake hands while maintaining eye contact and smiling. Some women do not shake hands and merely nod their head, so it is best to wait for a woman to extend her hand. Men may kiss a woman they know well on the cheek in place of a handshake. Greetings are leisurely and include time for social discussion and

exchanging pleasantries. Remember:
● DO shake hands upon meeting someone and don't forget to smile! Sometimes men may place their hand on the other person's shoulder during a handshake.
● DO shake hands again upon departing.
● DON'T shake hands with a woman unless she initiates it.
● DO exchange hugs and kisses with people you know well.
● DO be aware that observant Muslims will not shake hands with the opposite sex.
● DO lower your eyes or bow when meeting an elder. This shows respect.
● DO inquire about the person's family and health when exchanging greetings.

Visiting Someone's Home

● DO understand that in Muslim homes sometimes the male visitors and hosts will not eat with the women.
● DO compliment your host's home and belongings, but don't overdo it. If you do, your host might feel obligated to give you the belonging you're complimenting.
● DON'T linger after a meal is over. Leave about 30 minutes after.

Business Meeting Etiquette

Appointments are necessary and should be made as far in advance as possible. It may be difficult to arrange meetings with senior level managers on short notice, although you may be able to do so with lower-level managers. It is often difficult to schedule meetings from mid December to mid January or the two weeks surrounding Easter, as these are prime vacation times. Personal relationships are important. The initial meeting is often used to establish a personal rapport and to determine if you are trustworthy. After a meeting, send a letter summarizing what was decided and the next steps. Remember:
● DON'T be late, but don't be surprised if your host is late or even reschedules. It's not meant to be disrespectful; however, as a guest to Nigeria, you should be on time and keep all appointments.
● DO engage in small talk. Chat about sports, current events, or even politics. Don't discuss religious conflicts.
● DO bring a small gift that costs less than $ 50. Pens or little knickknacks are fine.
● DON'T use first names until invited to. Address people by their title and surname.
● DON'T give or receive business cards with your left hand.
● DO examine a business card that is given to you before putting it away.
● DON'T try to make a deal that sounds to good to be true. It will likely also sound suspicious.

Business Negotiation

It is imperative to develop mutual trust before negotiating. Women have yet to attain senior level positions. If you send a woman, she must expect to encounter some condescending behavior and to be tested in ways that a male colleague would not. Do not interrupt a South African while they are speaking.

South Africans strive for consensus and win-win situations.

- Include delivery dates in contracts. Deadlines are often viewed as fluid rather than firm commitments.
- Start negotiating with a realistic figure. South Africans do not like haggling over price. Decision-making may be concentrated at the top of the company and decisions are often made after consultation with subordinates, so the process can be slow and protracted.

Communication Etiquette

- DON'T use slang or profanity.
- DO note that people who live in the south of Nigeria speak louder and more directly.
- DO be aware that in the southwest of Nigeria, where the Yoruba tribe resides, they use a lot of proverbs and humor throughout conversation.
- DO understand that Nigerians communicate with a lot of gestures and body language, so you may have to pay attention to non-verbal cues when conversing.
- DON'T make generalizations about religion in Nigeria. Nigeria is a religiously diverse country, so it's important to understand that and maintain an open mind.
- DO be careful about eye contact. Constant and direct eye contact can be seeing as being intrusive.
- DON'T use your left hand to give or receive objects.

≫ 4. Business Etiquette in Egypt

Egypt is a country with a famously long and rich cultural history. Egyptians are considered to be extremely friendly gregarious and hospitable people. Family, honor and religion are of utmost importance to Egyptians. So a major consideration when visiting Egypt is that the main religion is Islam — although Christianity is also practiced — and much of the social customs and etiquette are influenced by this fact.

Dressing Etiquette

When visiting Egypt, you should be mindful of what is considered to be the most appropriate attire. Although within the confines of a resort, Western beachwear such as bikinis, shorts and miniskirts are generally accepted, when venturing outside you should always make sure that you are suitably dressed.

Women should always dress modestly. This means that skirts should be at least below the knee, and shoulders and the tops of arms should be covered. Men should wear trousers and also always have their shoulders covered. If you are planning on visiting a mosque, be aware that women will have to completely cover themselves, with only their face, hands and feet on display. A headscarf should also be worn. Also remember that if entering a mosque both men and women should remove their shoes. Not doing so would be seen as a complete and utter insult, and could cause quite a commotion.

Communication Etiquette

It is very important to understand the way in which you are expected to interact with members of the same and opposite sex when in Egypt. For instance, you should not kiss or make any body contact with a member of the opposite sex. Although handshakes may be offered, in contrast to Western customs, hugging and kissing on the cheeks is however, a common greeting between members of the same sex in Egypt. Egyptians also retain a close personal space between the same sexes, but you should avoid standing too close to the opposite sex. Men should also be aware that it is not always appropriate to idly chat with or approach an unknown Muslim woman.

Any displays of affection should be kept to an absolute minimum in public. Any displays of affection between same sex couples, particularly men, should be completely avoided. Outwardly flirtatious behavior is regarded as crass and immoral.

As Islam is the major religion of Egypt, and this means that certain foods and substances will be avoided by devout Muslims. These include alcohol, any drugs and pork. In the more touristy areas Egyptians will not be wholly offended if you choose to drink alcohol in their presence. However, it is good etiquette to only drink moderately in these circumstances.

Gesticulating & Body Language

You should be aware that in Egypt, showing the soles of your feet or shoes is perceived as very rude and bad etiquette. If you must make a refusal to an Egyptian's request, by putting your right hand over your heart, you are making an extremely polite rejection. The hand over the heart is a symbol of both humbleness and gratitude.

Although Egyptians are not superstitious people, for some the palm indicates the warding off of evil. Outside of some Egyptian's homes, you may see statues of hands with an eye painted into the palm, facing outwards. The idea is that the palm will ward off evil or the "envious" eye and protect the home. For this reason, if you are seen to push or wave your palms in an Egyptian's face, this could be considered as terrible etiquette, as it indicates that you regard them as evil or bad.

Dining Etiquette

When dining in Egypt, you should only use your right hand. Egyptians are extremely hospitable, and will put on quite a feast for you. You may find that even though you've finished eating, your Egyptian host will keep offering you food. They will be keen to make sure that you are properly tended to, but the repeated offers are also in part due to the custom of declining any offer at least once. If you are full, it is good etiquette to continually graciously decline their offers until they are satisfied that you are really are full.

Gift-giving Etiquette

In Egypt, give gifting is quite common, especially when visiting the homes of an Egyptian. You should try to avoid giving flowers, as these are retained for occasions such as weddings and funerals. More appropriate gifts include a high-quality compass (as it will allow a Muslim to always be directed to Mecca), sweets and chocolate, or any digital gadgetry. When giving or receiving a gift, you should only use your right or both hands.

≫ 5. Business Etiquette in Kenya

Kenya is a truly magnificent African country with its vast wildlife national reserves, awesome landscapes, beautiful beaches and friendly countrymen. Kenyans are very proud of their country, and are known to be very welcoming and warm people. When getting in touch with people in Kenya, you should be aware of what is considered to be proper etiquette so that you properly interact and integrate into Kenyan society, making the most of your stay.

Kenyans are quite conservative in their approach to social customs and etiquette in both the Christian and Muslim sectors of their society. However, more built-up urban areas such as the country's capital, Nairobi, tend to be more accepting and lenient towards alternative lifestyles and customs. You should also bear in mind that this is the opposite for the more rural locations.

You may notice that Kenyan people are also relatively mild-mannered and extremely polite, and so will admire these qualities in others. Always be prepared to offer your thanks and use "please" whenever possible — good, basic etiquette will earn you a great deal of respect as far as a Kenyan person is concerned.

Meeting Etiquette

Kenya is home to a number of ethnic groups, each with their own greeting customs. It is best to find out these customs before meeting with any particular group, so as to communicate that you are a respectful and well-informed individual. However, in most circumstances when meeting a Kenyan, smiling and handshaking are usual, although the handshake may be light compared to the firm, solid handshakes you might be used to. To show respect to a superior, you may hold your right forearm with the left hand whilst shaking their hand.

If traveling with children, be conscious that greetings between your child and a senior person may differ slightly. Your child should greet an elderly person with a small bow, which is then met with the flat of the elder's palm placed on the child's head.

In Kenya, it is considered proper etiquette to always shake hands with the right hand, as left-handed handshakes, as well as giving a gift with just your left hand, is considered wholly inappropriate.

In some cases, eye contact during formal introductions is minimal. This should not be construed as shyness or shiftiness; moreover it is a sign of respect and courtesy. You should therefore make sure to avoid making prolonged and direct eye contact when meeting and making introductions in Kenya. This could be interpreted as fairly intimidating or slightly disrespectful behavior. However, in most other situations, a degree of direct eye contact and smiling will help to inspire trust and sincerity.

Dressing Etiquette

In line with their common conservative ethos, Kenyans also tend to dress quite modestly. When traveling through Kenya, women especially should cover their shoulders and upper arms, particularly when in Muslim areas.

Men would be best to opt for (cotton or linen) trousers with a shirt or T-shirt, and women should wear longer skirts and dresses, with a modest and unrevealing top. Again, women especially should avoid wearing shorts, although in particularly well-populated tourist areas, this is generally deemed as acceptable

Beachwear such as bikinis and swimming trunks are accepted, so long as such attire is confined to the beach only.

Social Behavior

It is regarded as very poor etiquette to partake in public displays of affection in Kenya, and is generally not tolerated at all between same-sex couples. Although this is not so much the case in more"Westernized"areas such as Nairobi, you should still be mindful that some might still find it offensive behavior.

When doing business in Kenya, also be aware that directly pointing at someone with your finger is considered quite rude. If you need to point or direct, generally a nod of the head or opening your whole hand in the general direction of the person is more appropriate. Likewise, a beckoning motion with the index finger is also deemed improper — again using your whole hand is a better alternative.

There is no doubt that you will want to take many pictures whilst on business or holiday in Kenya. If you wish to include a person in your photographs, it is considered proper etiquette to politely ask them beforehand. Taking a picture without consent is considered very rude and will be frowned upon.

参考书目

金正昆．商务礼仪．北京：北京大学出版社，2004

金正昆．涉外礼仪教程．北京：中国人民大学出版社，2006

Robert，M. *HOW TO WIN ANY NEGOTIATION*. London：Career Press，2006

Cotton，D. 体验商务英语 2—3 册（*Market Leader* 2—3）．北京：高等教育出版社，2005

张立玉，王红卫．实用商务英语谈判．北京：北京理工大学出版社，2006

张立玉．实用商务礼仪．北京：北京理工大学出版社，2009

王强．服装专业英语．北京：化学工业出版社，2007

常跃进．现代交往英语口语．大连：大连理工大学出版社，2007

Crandell，A，许卉艳译．100 *Topics for Business English Situation*. 北京：外文出版社，2007

Williams，A. *Pass Cambridge BEC Preliminary*. 北京：经济科学出版社，2002

浩瀚．礼仪英语．北京：国防工业出版社，2007

张迪．休闲社交篇．北京：国防工业出版社，2006

陈冠蓓．时尚生活英语．青岛：青岛出版社，2006

吕维霞，刘彦波．现代商务礼仪．北京：对外经济贸易大学出版社，2003

李洪涛，潘永亮．美容化装．上海：上海科技出版社，2007

图书在版编目(CIP)数据

国际商务礼仪/张立玉著 . —武汉:武汉大学出版社,2014.9
国际商务系列教材
ISBN 978-7-307-13462-1

Ⅰ.国…　Ⅱ.张…　Ⅲ.国际商务—礼仪—高等学校—教材　Ⅳ.F718

中国版本图书馆 CIP 数据核字(2014)第 119163 号

责任编辑:谢群英　　责任校对:汪欣怡　　版式设计:韩闻锦

出版发行:**武汉大学出版社**　(430072　武昌　珞珈山)
　　　　　(电子邮件:cbs22@ whu.edu.cn 网址:www.wdp.com.cn)
印刷:湖北省京山德兴印务有限公司
开本:787×1092　1/16　印张:12　字数:280 千字　插页:1
版次:2014 年 9 月第 1 版　　2014 年 9 月第 1 次印刷
ISBN 978-7-307-13462-1　　定价:25.00 元